FOR EVERY SEASON

An introspective guide
to renewing ourselves
during the High Holidays and
throughout the Jewish Year

by

JEFF BERNHARDT

BLACKBIRD BOOKS

NEW YORK • LOS ANGELES

A Blackbird Original, July 2015

Manufactured in the United States of America.

Cataloging-in-Publication Data

For every season : An introspective guide to renewing ourselves during
the high holidays and throughout the Jewish year / by Jeff Bernhardt.
p. cm.
1. High Holidays—Study and teaching. 2. High Holidays—Meditations.
3. Fasts and feasts—Judaism—Exercises, recitations, etc. I. Title.
BM693.H5 B47 2015 296.4'31—dc22 2015942293

Blackbird Books
www.bbirdbooks.com
email us at editor@bbirdbooks.com

ISBN 978-1-61053-036-1

First Edition

10 9 8 7 6 5 4 3 2 1

Ben Zoma said: Who is wise? One who learns from every person; as it is said, "From each of those who have taught me, I have gained understanding." (Psalms 119:99)
Pirkei Avot (Ethics of Our Ancestors) 4:1

To My Teachers:
For everyone who has taught me by word or deed,
in the classroom and by example.

TABLE OF CONTENTS

Introduction: The Gift of Elul ix

Daily Reflections, Days 1–26...5

Intermezzo: *Teshuvah, Tefillah, Tzedakah*.....................109

Daily Reflections, Days 27–40...119

Shehecheyanu 175

Continuing the Journey..176

Chazak Chazak V'nitchazek...221

Acknowledgements...225

About the Author 227

Introduction: The Gift of Elul

When I was in my freshman year of college, I took an Environmental Sciences class. I dutifully showed up for the 9 AM class on Mondays, Wednesdays, and Fridays and had my pick of a seat in the large lecture hall. There were probably ten or more seats available for every student present. I couldn't understand why we were meeting in such a large space.

On the day of the midterm exam, I showed up for class a few minutes before it was to begin, and only then I understood. The room was filled with faces I had never seen before. I searched out a place to sit (made more difficult because we had to sit every other seat for the exam), and I surveyed the lecture hall which was, on *this* day, very well populated.

In more ways than one, the High Holidays are like midterm exams. On the High Holidays, there is often not a seat to be found in the sanctuary. Many synagogues have reserved seating to ensure that everyone has a seat and that it is a seat which is of his or her choosing. Many synagogue communities are unable to accommodate everyone, so they have an early and a late service or they relocate to a larger setting for the Days of Awe. Some have two simultaneous services on-site, if they have facilities which can accommodate this.

The High Holidays are like our spiritual midterm exams. And it wasn't until I was in my thirties that I realized their potential.

Until sometime during my fourth decade, I struggled with the idea of the High Holidays. Prior to that year, the High Holidays didn't speak to me—repetitive prayers, endless sermons, standing and sitting. Like so many others, I would attend the prayer services of the High Holidays hoping to be transformed. I hoped the prayers, the music of the choir, the sermons, something, *anything*, would move me. Often it felt like a very passive experience. Until that year, I expected to be transformed, but I was not engaged in my own process of transforming. Until that year, I hadn't realized that I had to actually *do* something if I wanted the holy days to mean something.

One year, my relationship to the High Holidays changed. I began to see them as filled with possibility and opportunity. That particular year, I took a class related to preparing for the High Holidays. As part of that class, each participant was provided some reflection materials to use prior to Rosh Hashanah. This is when I realized that, like with a midterm exam, if you don't prepare, you don't get as much out of it.

What I have learned is that if I don't put in the time prior to those prayer services, it is significantly less likely that they will help me experience a transformation. It is my responsibility to assess what it is I want to transform and to reflect and take actions toward those ends. The prayers, the sermons, and the music are our tools. They are for our use, but they cannot take the place of our own intentional efforts.

And that is why, I believe, we are given the gift of Elul, the month in the Hebrew calendar just prior to the High Holidays. It is a period for us to set aside some time to begin the introspection and reflection which these days call upon us to do.

There are rituals that some observe which are meant to help us to do this. It is the tradition in some communities to sound the shofar every morning of Elul (with the exception of Shabbat). This is the wake-up call, the symbolic alarm clock that reminds us that Rosh Hashanah is coming. A daily psalm is added to prayer services beginning in Elul. *Selichot* (special prayers for forgiveness) are added by Sephardic communities beginning in Elul and by Ashkenazic communities usually on the Saturday night prior to Rosh Hashanah.

The purpose of *this* text is to help each of us prepare for the High Holidays, for our personal midterm exams, exams that our tradition provides as a gift each year, an opportunity built into the Jewish calendar to reflect on our lives, on our relationships, on what we can each do to become the person that we know deep inside we have the potential to be.

Reflections on Sin

Al Chet ("for the Sin") is a part of the confessional which we recite repeatedly on Yom Kippur. For those of us who tend to be hard on ourselves, it is not difficult to go to that place where we beat our chests on the High Holidays for coming up short. It may be that we are simply not doing the things we know we should be doing, such as spending more quality time with our children, our aging parents, or our ill friends. We may beat ourselves up for not being more generous, or for not being as forgiving as we would like, or perhaps for losing patience or holding a grudge longer than we would like. And then there are those things for which we may feel especially guilty and may feel are actually sinful: stealing, being dishonest about how we spend our time at work, or lying to our loved ones.

A more gentle and less judgmental way to think about these actions is to consider that we are "missing the mark." In archery, the mark is the bull's-eye. In our lives, most of us aspire to hit the metaphoric bull's-eye. We want to be the best person we can be, but we know that we fall short, all of us. If an individual doesn't believe that he or she misses the mark at least sometimes, then my point has been made. After all, there are no exemptions for Yom Kippur, the day when we are each called upon to show up and answer for ourselves.

The challenge of the holy days is to look at our lives and to be brutally honest with ourselves. What are the things that I want to change? It may be how I treat others or how I behave in my inter-personal relationships. It may be how I interact in God's world (vis-à-vis the environment, for example), or it may be how I treat myself. Some of us are so hard on ourselves that it makes sense to resolve to be gentler.

Avivah Zornberg, a contemporary Israeli Torah scholar, teaches that we are each created with the *potential* of being in God's image. We are each a work in progress. Perhaps these holy days are a metaphoric midterm progress report: How am I doing in the following areas: Patience, dedication, integrity, humility? Perhaps the goal of the rest of the year is to improve those "grades."

Imagine these holy days as a parent-teacher conference, but you are the parent *and* the teacher *and* the student as well. What is it you need to work on? What tangible goals will you set forth, and how will you work toward those goals? How can you check in with yourself on your progress during the course of the year?

Next year will bring new goals and areas on which to focus, but it will also bring the opportunity to reflect back on what you will have achieved during the upcoming year. The intention of this text is to be a resource to help on the journey towards setting this year's goals and towards attaining them.

Using this Text

This text is meant to help each of us prepare for the reflection and introspection of the High Holidays. It can be used in the way that works best for you. Each page focuses on a liturgical or scriptural text that is part of the High Holiday prayer services. Several of these liturgical texts are also part of our daily prayer services, and their themes are particularly resonant during these holy days. While the readings are generally sequenced in the order in which we come upon them in the *machzor* (High Holiday prayerbook), they can certainly be reflected upon in any order.

There are questions after each text and its commentary, followed by pages for journaling. You can use that space to answer the questions provided or to expound upon your own ideas concerning the theme for that day.

In the liturgy of the High Holidays, we read that *teshuvah* (repentance or return), *tefillah* (prayer), and *tzedakah* (acts of righteousness) have the power to avert the severity of the decree. There is a section of this book which invites the reader to reflect on each of these three central themes and explore how these values are a part of our lives. There is an opportunity to think about how we might bring meaning to our lives through a more intentional commitment to these values.

Following the forty readings and journaling pages, representing the month of Elul and the Ten Days of Awe, are monthly opportunities to revisit and re-examine one's commitments.

It is often particularly challenging to carry our intentions from the sacred and awe-filled holy days into the rest of the year. This book offers guided opportunities to do this so that when we each enter the High Holidays next year, we can reflect on a year in which we have moved closer to becoming the person we hope to be, the person that we pray we can become during the Days of Awe.

This book, like the High Holidays, offers the opportunity to be used as a private, individual experience, as part of an intentional community, or, like our prayer services, it can be used both privately and communally. You may wish to use it as part of a discussion group, perhaps meeting weekly three or four times prior to the holy days and then on a monthly basis to explore some of the themes and challenges we face as we try to remain focused and committed to our goals as the year proceeds. *Rosh Chodesh* (the celebration of the new month in the Hebrew calendar) may serve as a good time each month to gather together for reflection, introspection, and communal support. No matter how you decide to proceed with the process of self-examination and renewal, let us begin!

FOR EVERY SEASON

לכל זמן ועת לכל חפץ תחת השמים :

עת ללדת ועת למות
עת לטעת ועת לעקור נטוע
עת להרוג ועת לרפוא
עת לפרוץ ועת לבנות
עת לבכות ועת לשחוק
עת ספוד ועת רכוד
עת להשליך אבנים ועת כנוס אבנים
עת לחבוק ועת לרחק מחבק
עת לבקש ועת לאבד
עת לשמור ועת להשליך
עת לקרוע ועת לתפור
עת לחשות ועת לדבר
עת לאהב ועת לשנא
עת מלחמה ועת שלום

To every thing there is a season,
And a time to every purpose under the heavens:

A time to be born, and a time to die;
A time to plant, and a time to pluck up that which is planted;
A time to kill, and a time to heal;
A time to break down, and a time to build up;
A time to weep, and a time to laugh;
A time to mourn, and a time to dance;
A time to cast away stones, and a time to gather stones together;
A time to embrace, and a time to refrain from embracing;
A time to seek, and a time to lose;
A time to keep, and a time to cast away;
A time to rend, and a time to sew;
A time to keep silence, and a time to speak;
A time to love, and a time to hate;
A time for war, and a time for peace.   (Ecclesiastes 3:1–6)

Day 1

1 Elul

הללויה

Halleluyah–Psalm 150

Praise the Eternal One in God's Holy Place
Praise the Eternal One in the Glorious Heavens
Praise the Eternal One for God's Mighty Acts
Praise the Eternal One for God's Overflowing Greatness
Praise the Eternal One with the shofar's blast
Praise the Eternal One with harp and lyre
Praise the Eternal One with drum and dance
Praise the Eternal One with strings and flute
Praise the Eternal One with resounding cymbals
Praise the Eternal One with resonant trumpets
Let every breath praise the Eternal One.
Praise the Eternal One.

This psalm is the last of the collection of psalms included in the Book of Writings, the last of the three books of the *Tanach*, the Jewish Bible. This psalm is recited every morning, all year. It is intentionally included in this book as the first reading for the Jewish month of Elul, because it teaches how we can be in relationship with God and how we can transform the everyday into the sacred. (The melody used in many synagogues is beautifully jubilant, but for an alternatively powerful melody, this psalm can be chanted to Leonard Cohen's "Hallelujah" melody).

This psalm paints an image as it extols and praises God. One can visualize, as one chants it, our ancestors singing, dancing, and playing musical instruments in ancient Jerusalem outside the Holy

Temple's walls. There is no judgment or concern that one is not singing in the right key or hitting all the notes. It is joyful—praising the Creator of Life. And, among the instruments, is the shofar!

From this psalm, we can see that there are many ways to praise God. There is a story of a young boy who does not know how to read Hebrew and therefore simply repeats over and over the letters of the Hebrew alphabet in the sincere hope that God will be able to put the letters together in the correct order. When a congregant scolds the boy for not chanting the prayers in the traditional manner, the rabbi chides the congregant, for the boy's prayer may not be traditional, but it flows from deep in his heart.

This is one of the messages of this psalm. Our relationship with God and our connection to God can be expressed in many ways—movement, dance, song, music, and traditional prayer—in any form which flows from our hearts. We can also understand from this prayer that we can make sacred every action we take. In Stephen Mitchell's modern interpretation, he writes:[1]

> . . . Praise God in market and workplace,
> with computer, with hammer and nails.
> Praise God in bedroom and kitchen;
> Praise God with pots and pans. . . .

When we recognize that every action, however mundane, has the potential of holiness, we raise the sanctity of our daily activities and relationships. We can consider the possibility of God's presence in *all* of our works and in *every* place in which we may reside. We have the ability to bring God in where we might not otherwise imagine God. As we are taught by Menachem Mendel of Kotzk: Where is God? Wherever we let God in.

---

[1] *A Book of Psalms*, Harper Perennial, 1994, p. 85.

In what ways do I praise God and communicate with God?

Are there other ways I might connect with God?

How might I approach my daily activities to be more mindful of the capacity they have for being sacred?

Day 2

2 Elul

בספר החיים

In the Book of Life

Remember us for life, Sovereign who delights in life; and inscribe us in the Book of Life for Your sake, God of Life.

This verse is added to the *Amidah* prayer for the High Holidays. On these holy days, we imagine God as judge. Each of us has a page in the Book of Life dedicated to our deeds. The hope is that the good we have done in the previous year will outweigh the bad and that we will be deemed worthy of being recorded in the Book of Life for another year. Each of us stands before the Judge of Judges and pleads our case, asking for mercy.

For most of us, while we can certainly be better people and do better in our lives and in our relationships, it is difficult to imagine that we merit anything but mercy. We can imagine God as the strict but merciful judge who wants each of us to become the best version of the person we are capable of becoming, who considers our potential and thus grants us another year on this earth to strive toward achieving that potential.

For many, God as judge and a Book of Life in which our deeds are recorded are challenging if not troubling images. One's concept of God may not take such a form, and the idea of a Book of Life creates a system in which punishment (in this case, death) is related to deeds. One is therefore being punished for "missing the mark." For many, this is not the concept of God that we embrace.

So, when we recite these prayers to God, asking to be remembered for life, begging for the mercy of the metaphoric court, pleading with God as judge, what might we have in mind? Perhaps we are beating our chests over our transgressions and pleading to our inner selves as we ache to be the person we know that we are capable of being. Yes, we long to be written in the Book of Life for another year, but perhaps this metaphoric page is like a mirror in which we stare at our reflection honestly and truly see ourselves. We feel regret for the ways we have missed the mark, and we commit to the potential that each of us knows is within our grasp.

As we reflect during these days, let us honestly look in the mirror and envision how we can become our best self.

In what ways have I managed to hit the mark, to be the best version of myself?

In what ways have I fallen short?

In what areas am I doing better than last year?

In what areas do I still have a way to go? Am I committed to make the effort?

Day 3

3 Elul

אב הרחמים

Merciful Parent

Who is like You, Merciful Parent? With compassion You remember Your creations for life.

This verse, like the verse from Day 2, is also an addition to the High Holiday Amidah. We imagine God as Sovereign (traditionally, King) and several verses later, as Parent (traditionally, Father). God is a parent who has mercy upon us—the opposite of the old saying, "Spare the rod, spoil the child." The God we imagine does not mete out harsh punishment but rather is a God of *rachamim,* a God who has mercy and compassion upon us. It is noteworthy, in this context, that in Hebrew, the word for "mercy" shares the same root as the word for "womb."

In the above liturgical verse we consider our relationship with and our conception of God. We reflect on God's qualities as well. Just as God's character and qualities are multifaceted, so is our relationship with God complex and multifaceted. Am I appealing to God as Parent or as Sovereign? Am I appealing to the God of Justice or to the God of Mercy? Am I appealing to my own desire or need to be merciful with myself?

One way to understand these and other prayers which invoke God's character is in the context of this verse found in Genesis 1:27: *And the Eternal One created human beings in God's own image, in the divine image God created him; male and female God created them.*

If I am created in the image of God, and God is, among other characteristics, merciful, then I too am ideally meant to be merciful—merciful with myself as well as in my relationships with those in my life.

Are there actions or deeds for which I hope God will be particularly merciful with me?

If so, what are those actions or deeds?

In what ways can I show greater compassion with myself and in my personal relationships? In my professional relationships? In my interactions with others with whom I cross paths?

Day 4

4 Elul

וכתוב

And Inscribe

And inscribe all the children of Your covenant for a good life.

This verse too is an addition to the High Holiday Amidah. If we take it at face value, how might we understand it? It seems that we are praying for the impossible, like praying for the recovery of a loved one with a chronic or terminal illness. Miracles may happen, and those with ultimate faith in an omnipotent God may certainly pray for what might seem impossible. However, how do we come to terms with prayer and God when our prayers seem to go unanswered or may be answered but not in the way we hope? And, when I pray for every one of God's children to have a good life, an outcome which seems unlikely, am I praying for the impossible? And furthermore, what defines a good life? While there may be some common characteristics, each of us likely has a different idea of what truly makes for a good life.

As does so much of the liturgy of the High Holidays, this one line in this one prayer raises many challenging questions. That being said, perhaps part of the goal of the liturgy is to bring us to this struggle. We are *Yisrael*—ones who wrestle with God.

One may wonder whether this verse and others like it may be calling to us and reminding us that *we* have a responsibility. It is not enough to pray for others to have a good life, however one may define it. More to the point, this verse may be reminding us that it is incumbent upon us to practice *tzedakah* (acts of righteousness), and *gemilut chasadim* (acts of lovingkindness), and to transform the

17

world into one in which there is the possibility of a good life for each individual and a world in which we actually consider our responsibility to others to ensure their good life.

A commentary on the narrative of Noah serves as an example. The text speaks of Noah as righteous "in his generation," rather than simply referring to him as righteous. The question is: why does the text add the qualifying phrase, "in his generation?" In an attempt to answer this question, one commentary explains that when it is cold, one can choose to put on a coat and simply warm oneself, or one can light a fire and warm everyone. By building an ark for his family alone rather than advocating on behalf of others, Noah chose to do the former.

So perhaps the question raised by the verse above is more about what each of us can do as God's partner to metaphorically keep one another warm. And perhaps that is what we are praying for, this insight and the strength to take action towards that end.

How do I wrestle with God? What do I find most challenging in this relationship? In the liturgy?

What role do I have in helping to ensure that others have a good life? Toward this end, what more could I do?

Day 5

5 Elul

לחיים טובים ולשלום

For a Good Life and for Peace

In the Book of Life, blessing, and peace, and good livelihood, may we and all Your people Israel be remembered and be written before You for a good life and for peace. Blessed are You, Eternal One, who makes Peace.

On the High Holidays, we add the above verse to the closing prayer of the Amidah. In addition, we make a slight change to the *chatimah* (the end of the blessing). During the year, we say: *Blessed are You, Eternal One, who blesses Your people with peace.*

This prayer (traditionally referred to as *Sim Shalom*—Grant Peace) asks God for peace in addition to other blessings.

The word *shalom* is commonly translated as *peace, hello,* or *goodbye.* There is an old quip: How do you know if someone means hello, goodbye, or peace? The response is that it depends if the person is walking toward you or away from you. But the deeper meaning of this seemingly simple word is found in its Hebrew root, which is the same as for the word *shalem,* "whole."

The broader interpretation is, therefore, that when we wish someone *shalom*—whether they are coming, going, or just simply staying put—we are wishing them a sense of wholeness, completeness, and inner peace; we are wishing for them to be at peace in their lives.

At the end of the Amidah, traditionally recited at least three times each day, we pray for wholeness for ourselves, our loved

ones, the Jewish people, and for the world. We pray to be remembered in the Book of Life for blessings.

In what way do I feel a sense of wholeness? What has brought me to feel this way?

In what way do I feel broken? What has brought me to feel this way?

How does this compare to how I felt a year ago? If there has been a change, what is the explanation for this shift?

As I pray to God for these blessings, what could be my role in bringing these blessings to my life and to my world?

Day 6

6 Elul

נצור לשוני מרע

Guard My Tongue from Evil

My God, guard my tongue from evil and my lips from speaking falsehood. And to those who curse me, may my soul be silent. . . . May the words of my heart and the meditations of my soul be acceptable to You, Eternal One, my Rock and my Redeemer.

This text is the closing meditation of the Amidah. It is not particular to the High Holidays, but it speaks to some of the challenges many of us may face during the Days of Awe as well as during the rest of the year. We strive to hit the mark; we aim to hit the bull's-eye in our behavior, in our way of being in the world. This prayer reminds and challenges us to work on what is perhaps one of the most difficult struggles we have as people: to use our words to bring peace rather than to cause harm, whether we do so intentionally or not. Among the confessionals we recite on Yom Kippur are some which involve our words and how we use them. In his book *Words that Hurt, Words that Heal*, Rabbi Joseph Telushkin reminds us of the many ways we use our words and how critical it is to be vigilant in our use of those words and to be aware of the power they have to harm as well as to heal.

When I think about the power of words, a personal memory comes to mind. As a novice educator, I once told a student that I was disappointed in him because of the way he behaved in a particular situation. This student and I shared a very positive relationship, but I didn't realize the extent to which our relationship mattered to him. I allowed my ego to get in the way, and I believed that because of his respect for me, my words could transform his behavior. I came to learn from the school counselor how devastating my comment was to this student. It was because of how much my opinion mattered to him that my words were so wounding. I did due diligence to repair that wound, and I learned my lesson. The words I used in an effort to help my student change his behavior were, albeit unintentionally, hurtful to him and to our relationship.

Just as words can be harmful, each of us has also been on the giving and receiving end of kind words. We know what it means to share sincere, unsolicited, caring words with a friend or a stranger. How often do we think these nice thoughts, but do not take the moment to share them, whether in a note, an email, a text, or a phone call? It can mean so much to know that someone is thinking about us.

How do I use words?

Have I used words in a way that may have done harm and which I can repair?

How can I better use my words in order to bring healing rather than harm?

What kind of commitment can I make to use my words to regularly show appreciation, gratitude, and goodwill?

Day 7

7 Elul

המלך

The King

The King sits upon a high and lofty throne.

This section of the Rosh Hashanah morning service is traditionally chanted in ever-increasing volume in order to emphasize that God (traditionally described as the King of the universe) is sitting in judgment. It dates back to the thirteenth century.

The idea of God as King may be a challenging image for a number of reasons. First off is the use of gender language when we refer to God in our prayers. Of course, God has no gender; therefore the default to the male gender can be off-putting and unintentionally limiting. On a day when we are focused on the challenge of deep introspection, the focus should be on the inner reflection rather than the distraction of the gender attributed to God due to the limitations of our language. While the Hebrew may remain unchanged in many *machzorim* (holiday prayerbooks), the translation used in some is often changed to reflect a more gender-neutral understanding of God, such as the Eternal One or Sovereign.

Another challenge is the image which may come to mind when we think of God as King, a word which conjures images of God sitting on a throne of judgment. This may carry its own burden. Much of the holy day liturgy is focused on this image of God sitting in judgment of each of us. At a time in the Jewish calendar when we are called to look inward, each of us will likely relate to this prayer in the context in which we imagine God. That Sovereign may be compassionate, merciful, just, or harsh.

29

HaMelech, "the King" or "the Sovereign," reminds us that this holiday is about judgment. Whether or not we believe that God is judging us, on these days, we are called upon to judge ourselves. Whether we think of it as our super-ego, our internal critic, or our conscience, we are called to look in the metaphoric mirror, into our own souls. We are called to ask ourselves the difficult questions and to challenge ourselves to face the sometimes difficult answers. And then we are called on to take action based on those sometimes gut-wrenching answers.

How will I judge myself during these days?

Will I mete out a harsh judgment or will I judge myself with compassion?

How will I forge the path which will help me to become the person I hope to be?

Day 8

8 Elul

ובכן

And Therefore

Uvchen:
And therefore place your awe . . . ,
And therefore grant honor . . . ,
And therefore the righteous will see and rejoice . . . .

The *Uvchen* ("And therefore") is one of the most ancient parts of the High Holiday service, believed to date back to the second century. It is part of the *Kedushah* section of the High Holiday Amidah. It is a three part prayer, each part beginning with the word Uvchen. It imagines a time when peace and righteousness will reign throughout the world and evil will vanish.

Rabbi Harold Schulweis, *z"l,* in his essay for *On Sacred Ground,* writes that *al ken* (also translated as *therefore* and related to the Hebrew word *uvchen*) is a critical word. He writes that it is the word that "lies at the edge of conscience," that it calls us to action. He summarizes its importance by writing, "Without *therefore,* the words remain the same, the world remains the same, I remain the same."

We implore God with the "and therefore," but we are the co-signers of the contract. We are partners with God in the creation and repair of the world. In Rabbi Marc Gellman's book of modern midrash, *Does God Have a Big Toe?,* his story titled "Partners" takes a humorous yet thought-provoking look at this idea.

"Partners" reminds us that we are, indeed, God's partners. The world may have been created by God in the traditional and literal reading, but it is incumbent upon each of us to continue the work. In a world filled with violence, war, inequality, disease, and homelessness, to name a few of the challenges we face as a global community, it is our obligation to partner with God and with one another to bring wholeness to our world. As an example, in the *Birkat haMazon,* the blessing after the meal, there is a verse which praises God for feeding everyone. We all know that not everyone has food, but is that because there isn't enough food or is that because we are not doing our share as God's partners to ensure that there is food for all?

Uvchen. And therefore.

I see the problem; *and therefore* what will I do about it? Will I take some action or will I allow myself and the world to remain the same?

As I reflect on my life and my role in the world, what is my part in bringing healing and wholeness, whether it be on a grand scale or in my small corner of the world?

In the coming year, how can I commit myself toward this goal?

Can seeing myself as a partner with God and acting on that idea impact how I see myself? If so, in what way?

Day 9

9 Elul

וּבְכֵן תֵּן פַּחְדְּךָ

And Therefore Place Your Awe

And therefore place Your awe, Eternal One our God, upon all whom You have made . . . .

In the first of the three *Uvchen* sections, we ask that God infuse us, God's creations, with awe of the Eternal One and with awe of God's world. We ask for God's help that we should do God's work in the world with a pure heart.

How thought-provoking that we ask in a prayer on these High Holidays for God's help to achieve a state of awe and to channel that to positive effect in the world. Awe is defined as a reverential respect that involves fear or wonder. In more modern colloquial language, we describe an experience as "awesome." This colloquial use of the term, however, may not really do justice to what it means to be in a state of awe.

How often are we truly in awe of another person's achievement, performance, or knowledge (or our own for that matter)? How often do we truly marvel in this deepest way at a natural wonder or at being present at a moment that we know has the capacity to impact our lives or to change history? How often do we truly recognize the awesomeness of what can be described as a miracle, that which is possibly beyond explanation?

The story is told that Rabbi Abraham Joshua Heschel, twentieth century scholar and activist, entered his classroom one day and declared to his students with ecstatic expression that he had witnessed a miracle that morning. When the students eagerly asked

37

what this miracle was, he declared that he woke up and realized that he was alive. What a reminder of the everyday awesome moments to which we so easily become desensitized!

Heschel reminds us that we experience moments of awe everyday, but do we recognize them? And once we recognize those moments as awe-filled, do we acknowledge them and do they bring us to praise God and recognize all that which is greater and beyond our understanding? How often does this recognition lead us to act?

In this prayer, we ask God to infuse us and everything beyond us with awe and with the awareness of that awe and to even somehow recognize the possibility that we may be changed by that awareness and by the experience itself.

Is there a moment or experience in this past year or in recent years which I can describe as *awesome*? What made it *awesome*?

What might I do to bring greater awareness into my life of the *awesomeness* which exists in the world and in the everyday?

Day 10

10 Elul

ובכן תן כבוד

And Therefore Grant Honor

And therefore, Eternal One, grant honor to Your people, glory to those in awe of You, hope to those who seek You, openness of speech to those who yearn for You, happiness to Your land, and gladness to Your city . . . .

In the second of the three *Uvchen* prayers, we pray for God to grant us honor, glory, and hope. We hope for the time of the Messiah to come, a time in which there will be peace in the world, a time when, according to the prophet Isaiah, "the wolf shall dwell with the lamb" (Isaiah 11:6), and "they shall beat their swords into plowshares and their spears into pruning hooks." (Isaiah 2:4)

There are different ideas within Judaism about the Messiah and what the Messiah represents. Judaism focuses on the here and now, but we do pray for the messianic age, a time when the world will be at peace and nations and their peoples will live with one another in peace.

One tradition states that the Messiah will come when every Jewish person observes two consecutive *Shabbatot*. This, of course, represents a particular worldview, but, by the same token, it underscores the idea that we can each play a role in bringing the messianic age, the time when people can live with one another in peace.

We ask God to grant honor to "Your people," glory to "those in awe of You," and hope to "those who seek You." So we acknowledge that we have a part to play in this contract. We ask these things of God, and we recognize that we are to be a reflection of God in the world.

How do I reflect God's presence in the world? In my relation-ships?

How can I bring the world closer to Isaiah's description of the messianic age?

What is it that I truly hope for?

Day 11

11 Elul

ובכן צדיקים

And Therefore the Righteous Will See and Rejoice

And therefore the righteous will see and rejoice, the upright will exult, and the compassionate will thrill with delight . . . .

The Hebrew word commonly used for charity is *tzedakah*. A better translation is "righteousness" or "an act of righteousness." We give to those in need because we are commanded to do so and because it is the right thing to do. Perhaps if we get into the habit of doing this, it will become natural to us. Other related words are *tzedek*, often translated as "justice," and *tzadik*, "a righteous individual."

There is a belief in Jewish folklore that in any given generation, there exist thirty-six righteous people (traditionally men), who, due solely to their merit, allow the world to exist. They are called *lamedvavniks* (the numerical equivalent of the Hebrew letters *lamed* and *vav* is thirty-six).

When we think of a tzadik, we may feel humbled and even intimidated. And if I consider myself a tzadik, then by virtue of the definition, I can now count myself out. A tzadik would not profess his or her own righteousness. He or she would simply live those ideals, and it would be manifested in his or her interactions and behaviors. The ideal of living a righteous life, a life in which our actions reflect our highest values, is a tall order.

The High Holidays call on us to look in the mirror and ask ourselves what we see. Just as the mezuzah may remind each of us to be the best person we can be, the liturgy of the High Holidays not only asks but compels us to face this question. It implores us to look ourselves in the mirror and ask whether we can truly say that we are the best version of ourselves.

This question is illustrated in a story about Rabbi Zusya. As he was dying, he said that he was afraid. When asked of what he was afraid, he responded: "When I die I am not afraid of being asked: *Why did you not act like Moses?* because I am not Moses. I am afraid of being asked: *Why did you not act more like Zusya?*"

It is incumbent upon each of us to be the best person that we can be. We do not have to measure ourselves by others but only by our own potential.

What does it mean to live a righteous life?

In what way am I leading a life that I would consider to be righteous?

What can I do to live a more righteous existence? What is the greatest challenge I face toward that end?

How can I live up to my own potential as opposed to measuring myself against someone else? How can I be more gentle with myself in this regard?

Day 12

12 Elul

אתה בחרתנו

You Have Chosen Us

You have chosen us from all of the peoples, You have loved us and desired us and have exalted us from all the languages, and You have made us holy with Your commandments, and You have brought us close to You to be in Your service and to call upon us by Your great and holy name.

In the Book of Deuteronomy 7:6, we read: "For you are a holy people to the Eternal One, your God. The Eternal One your God has chosen you to be God's own treasure, out of all peoples that are on the face of the earth."

What does it mean to be chosen? And what does it mean in regard to our relationship with other peoples, presumably the unchosen? Some understand this as being chosen to fulfill the commandments, chosen to be responsible to God's commandments. For others, this concept of being chosen means to be "a light unto the nations," to live by example. Needless to say, it is difficult enough to be the best person that one can be, let alone the best person representing an entire people.

Many of us have reacted in shame when one of our people makes the front page of the newspaper for some nefarious act. By the same token, we feel proud of our disproportionate number of Nobel laureates. But this merely underscores the point that whichever interpretation we use—whether we are leading by example as "a light unto the nations" or simply being good citizens, fulfilling God's commandments—each of us has a responsibility as individuals to be a positive role model. Just as others affect us, we affect the world.

Do I feel an obligation to be a role model? How? For whom?

Who are my role models? What values and achievements do I seek to emulate?

Do I feel an obligation to represent the Jewish people in a positive light in my interactions with others? In what way? Is this a burden or a responsibility that I feel or take upon myself? Why?

Day 13

13 Elul

יום תרועה

A Day for Blowing the Shofar

Eternal One, our God, You have given to us with love this Day of Remembrance, a day for the blowing of the shofar, a holy time in remembrance of the Exodus from Egypt.

The Exodus from Egypt is a seminal event in Jewish history and consciousness. So much of our holiday cycle revolves around it, as do our values. Sukkot and Passover are intimately tied to re-membering the lives of our ancestors and how with God's help, they made the physical, emotional, and psychological journey from slav-ery to freedom. Our rituals, like dwelling in the sukkah or eating matzah, are meant to remind us of our ancestors' journey and to in-still in us the sensory memories which call upon us to feel that it is *our* journey as well, our exodus. The Torah, in fact, repeatedly im-plores us not to oppress the stranger, for we know the heart of the stranger, as we were strangers ourselves in Egypt.

So, yet again, in this prayer, we are reminded of the Exodus and that this festival of Rosh Hashanah is also intrinsically tied to the Exodus.

What, then, is the connection between the Day of Judgment and the Exodus? What exactly are we being called upon to remem-ber?

Perhaps the key is in the sounding of the shofar, referred to in the liturgical verse above. Not only are the blasts a celebration of our physical freedom from enslavement in Egypt, they are also a call to us to be spiritually free as well, to cast off the metaphorical chains that bind us and to thereby awaken us to our own potential. Just as on Passover when we collect and burn our *chametz* and symbolically discharge those things which enslave us in our lives, at the *tashlich* service, traditionally observed on Rosh Hashanah, we cast away those sins which weigh us down.

What weighs me down?

What can I do to cast off these symbolic chains?

What is my spiritual journey? What is my personal exodus narrative?

Day 14

14 Elul

אבינו מלכנו

Avinu Malkeinu: Our Father, Our King

Our Father, Our King be gracious to us and answer us though we have no merits; be charitable towards us, acting with kindness, and save us.

Mentioned in the Talmud, this final verse of *Avinu Malkeinu* is one of the hallmarks of the High Holiday liturgy. In the ninth century prayerbook of Rav Amram Gaon, Avinu Malkeinu consists of twenty-five verses. Since that time, various communities have added to it to reflect the disasters and persecutions that have befallen them. In recent decades, some communities have adopted an abridged version. Some modern versions have also opted for more gender-neutral language.

Traditional communities do not recite Avinu Malkeinu on Shabbat, because in the prayer we request from God healing, sustenance, and other needs, and it is customary on Shabbat not to focus on the absence of these things and thereby cause ourselves greater distress.

The verses of Avinu Malkeinu include our acknowledgement that we have transgressed and that God is our only Sovereign. We implore God to grant forgiveness and mercy as well as innumerable favors and kindnesses. We pray for healing, for pardon, and to spare us from the harm that our adversaries might cause us. We pray for blessings, for mercy for our children and for those who have died.

Despite additions and edits to the prayer, the final verse remains. Its melody serves as one of the sensory memories most associated with the liturgy of these holy days. It is the imploring of God, our Parent and our Sovereign, to spare us and to act kindly for our sake, for the sake of those who came before us, and for God's sake.

We are in essence throwing ourselves on the mercy of the court. The words of this final verse raise the question: Do we not have merits?

Of course we do. But here we are at our most vulnerable, pleading for compassion, that God should give us the benefit of the doubt, that God should see that the scale is tipped in our favor, or perhaps God should even tip it in our favor.

What are my merits?

If I were pleading for compassion and kindness from God, what arguments would I make on my own behalf? Not excuses. Not defenses of my actions. But what would I ask of God, the ultimate Parent figure?

What is it that I am actually asking of God at this moment? What is it that I most want? What would that look like?

Day 15

15 Elul

פקד את שרה

The Eternal One Remembered Sarah

And The Eternal One remembered Sarah as God had said; and the Eternal One did for Sarah as God had spoken.

The traditional Torah reading for the first day of Rosh Hashanah is the narrative of the birth of Isaac. According to tradition, it is read on Rosh Hashanah, because God *remembered* Sarah on the first day of Rosh Hashanah, Isaac's birthday. The reading is found in Genesis 21:1–34.

In this narrative, shortly after the birth of Isaac to Abraham and Sarah who are well past the age of conceiving a child, Sarah tells Abraham that she wants her servant, Hagar, and Hagar's son, Ishmael, Abraham's first born, to be cast out of their midst into the wilderness. This would clearly place them in danger. Abraham reluctantly relents after reassurance from God that Ishmael and Hagar will survive and that Ishmael will become the father of a nation because he too is Abraham's son.

It is striking that the Torah reading chosen for this holy day includes such a troubling action taken by Sarah, one of our revered matriarchs. On the one hand, she can be seen as protecting her own child. On the other hand, she can be seen as heartlessly casting out her husband's first born along with his mother. It is clear that there is distress about this. Hagar is so worried about what may come that she assumes that Ishmael will die of thirst and cannot bear to witness this.

61

While we read that Abraham is troubled by Sarah's action, one wonders whether Sarah felt regret or guilt after the fact.

Sarah's action may be extreme, but what might we learn from the inclusion of this reading on the first day of Rosh Hashanah? Perhaps it is meant to remind us that even our patriarchs and matriarchs were human and sometimes subject to emotional responses to situations rather than acting in a more charitable way, in a manner more reflective of their higher selves. Perhaps it is meant to remind us that every one of us, Sarah included, can strive to be a better person even when it may mean that we will have to suffer a bit by putting our egos aside.

When have I been faced with a dilemma and struggled to take the high road despite my inclination to do otherwise?

Did I take the high road or did I choose to follow my initial impulse? Did I regret that choice? Did it impact how I felt about myself afterwards?

How can I use this to help me do *teshuvah,* to return to the right path?

Day 16

16 Elul

ועשיתם עלה

And You Shall Prepare an Offering

And in the seventh month, on the first day of the month, you shall have a holy convocation: you shall do no manner of servile work; it is a day of blowing the horn to you. And you shall prepare a burnt-offering for a sweet savor to the Eternal One: one young bullock, one ram, seven he-lambs of the first year without blemish; and their meal-offering, fine flour mingled with oil, three tenth parts for the bullock, two tenth parts for the ram, and one tenth part for every lamb of the seven lambs; and one he-goat for a sin-offering, to make atonement for you; beside the burnt-offering of the new moon, and the meal-offering thereof, and the continual burnt-offering and the meal-offering thereof, and their drink-offerings, according to their ordinance, for a sweet savor, an offering made by fire to the Eternal One.

The *maftir* (additional *aliyah*) for both days of Rosh Hashanah is taken from Numbers 29:1–6. The text addresses the biblical offerings for this holy day. There are many verses in the Torah which focus on offerings or sacrifices. The Hebrew word for "offering" or "sacrifice" is *korban*, which shares the Hebrew root for "near" or "next to." In ancient times this was a way the people felt close to God. Either agricultural products or livestock, different offerings were prescribed for different occasions—peace, thanksgiving, free will, guilt, and sin—and there were different procedures to be followed for each.

While these specific rituals may not be relevant today, the underlying meaning is as important as ever: Sacrificing something of great value in order to get closer to God and to strengthen our relationship to God.

We are also called to ask how, in a world without the biblical offerings, we can feel closer to God's presence. For each of us this may be different, though the Jewish tradition provides some ways we can achieve this. We can offer additional prayers to God. We may choose to observe the commandments, celebrate the holidays and Shabbat, and perform acts of *tzedakah* and *gemilut chasadim* (acts of lovingkindness).

What do I do in my life to feel close to God and my Judaism? Does this bring me closer to God's presence?

Is there a Jewish ritual I have wanted to bring into my life?

What might I add to my life that would help me to feel closer to God?

Am I at peace with the sacrifices I have made in my life? If not, what can I do to be at peace?

Day 17

17 Elul

ותתפלל חנה

And Hannah Prayed

And Hannah prayed and said: My heart exults in the Eternal One, my glory is exalted in the Eternal One; my mouth is enlarged over my enemies; because I rejoice in Your salvation. There is none holy as the Eternal One, for there is none beside You; neither is there any Rock like our God.

The *haftarah* (selection from the Book of Prophets) that is traditionally chanted on the first day of Rosh Hashanah is from First Samuel (1:1–2:10). This selection is a recounting of the story of Hannah, who is barren and prays for a son. Her prayer is answered, and Samuel is born. After he is born and later weaned, she fulfills her promise to God and gives him up to serve God for his lifetime. This excerpt from the Book of Prophets is traditionally read on Rosh Hashanah, as, according to tradition, this is when God *remembered* Hannah. It parallels the Torah reading for the first day of Rosh Hashanah, in which God remembers Sarah on Rosh Hashanah.

Other themes from Rosh Hashanah reverberate in the haftarah: The fervent praying of Hannah, the prayer which ends the haftarah in which she extols God as the God of Justice and the idea of being remembered by God (mirrored in the Rosh Hashanah *Zichronot* service).

Hannah's fervent prayers to God are seen as a model for our silent prayers today. In the haftarah, Hannah prays to God for a son. We read that her lips moved, but no words could be heard. Eli, the priest, presumes that she is drunk. She explains that what he sees is not due to intoxication but due to the angst that she feels at not having been able to conceive a child. She models the private prayer that we are each encouraged to include in our own prayers. Our sages go so far as to say that our prayers are not complete if they do not include the prayers of our hearts.

At this time in the cycle of our holy days, our hearts are filled with fervent prayers like those in Hannah's heart.

What is the role of prayer in my life?

For what do I pray to God? Do I have an expectation of myself and my own role in making those prayers become a reality?

How do I come to terms with my relationship with God if those prayers seem to go unanswered?

Day 18

18 Elul

עקידת יצחק

The Binding of Isaac

And it came to pass after these things, that God did test Abraham and said to him: "Abraham;" and he said: "Here am I." And God said: "Take now your son, your only son, Isaac, whom you love, and go to the land of Moriah; and offer him there for a burnt-offering upon one of the mountains which I will tell you of."

The Torah reading traditionally chanted on the second day of Rosh Hashanah is that of the *Akeidah* (Genesis 22:1–24). This narrative is one of the most difficult in the Torah. Abraham, the first Jew, chosen by God to be the father of our people, is told by God to offer up his son Isaac, the son he shares with Sarah, the miracle child of their old age.

The commentaries and discussions about this narrative and the consequences it holds for all of the personalities in the text are countless. In the telling, we, the "audience," know what is about to happen, and we know how it ends. We are moved by Isaac's innocence as he asks his father, "Here is the fire and the wood, but where is the lamb for a burnt-offering?" We react with a chill to Abraham's response: "God will provide the lamb for a burnt-offering, my son." Does Abraham have faith that in the end God will provide a substitute for his son? Is he the faithful servant? Is he the protective father, hiding the painful, awful truth?

We know the ending of the narrative, but we come face-to-face with the most difficult question. How can God ask this of Abraham and how can Abraham agree?

It is interesting that this text follows the Torah reading selected for the first day of Rosh Hashanah. In the traditional Torah reading from the first day, Sarah throws Hagar and Ishmael into the wilderness and to whatever dangers might await them. On the second day, we read of Abraham's willingness to sacrifice his son. In the first, Abraham is reassured by God, and in the second, God reassures Abraham with the substitution of the ram—but not before Abraham is holding the knife above Isaac.

Perhaps, like the first day's reading, this is to remind us of the humanness of the biblical personalities we hold up with such high esteem. Perhaps it is to remind us of their blind spots. Perhaps it is to remind us that we have the potential to rise to our higher selves. Perhaps it is simply to remind us of the importance of having faith.

How am I like Abraham and like Sarah in struggling with moral dilemmas?

What does it mean to me to have faith?

What role does faith play in my life?

In what or in whom do I have faith? In what or whom don't I have faith?

Would I like to see the role of faith in my life change in some way? How?

Day 19

19 Elul

ואהבת עולם אהבתיך

With Everlasting Love, I Love You

Thus says the Eternal One: The people that were left of the sword have found grace in the wilderness, even Israel, when I go to cause him to rest.

From afar, the Eternal One appeared to me, saying: "With everlasting love, I love you; therefore with affection have I drawn you to me . . . ."

The haftarah for the second day of Rosh Hashanah is taken from the prophetic book, Jeremiah 31:2–20.

In the haftarah, we read that God says: *With everlasting love I love you; therefore with affection have I drawn you to me . . . Again I will build you and you shall be restored . . . Again you shall plant vineyards on the hills of Samaria; the planters shall plant and enjoy the fruit.*

The text continues: *. . . their soul shall be as a watered garden . . . I will turn their mourning into gladness, and I will comfort them, and make them rejoice from their sorrow . . . My people shall be filled with My goodness, says the Eternal One.*

The tone and mood of the haftarah is one of hope and of faith. God, through the words of the prophet, is offering comfort to the people with the assurance that Israel will be restored and preserved.

When, towards the end of the haftarah, the matriarch Rachel is said to be crying from her grave over the fate of the children of

Israel, she is assured and comforted that "your children shall return to their own land."

This haftarah is one of hope for the future. It is meant to reassure the children of Israel that they will be lovingly returned to the Holy Land. On the day when this text is traditionally chanted, we are in the midst of prayer and hope for a good year to come for ourselves, for our loved ones, and for our community. We read Jeremiah's message and can be comforted by his words of hope and faith.

What are my hopes for the new year?

What are my fears?

What or who gives me strength as I enter the future, the unknown?

How does God give me hope and strength to face the unknown?

Day 20

20 Elul

תקיעת שופר

The Sounding of the Shofar

Blessed are You, Eternal One our God, Sovereign of the universe, who has made us holy with Your commandments and has commanded us to hear the sound of the shofar.

There are many reasons given for the sounding of the *shofar* on Rosh Hashanah. As mentioned earlier, in some communities, it is sounded every day (with the exception of Shabbat) in the Hebrew month of Elul. The Torah commands us to commemorate the day with "loud blasts" (Leviticus 23:24) but does not specifically mention the shofar. So the question is not only *why* we mark this day with "loud blasts," but why the shofar?

While there are many explanations for the sounding of the shofar on Rosh Hashanah, a particularly resonant one is found in the connection to our Rosh Hashanah scriptural readings: The sounds of the shofar remind us of the desperate wails of Sarah and Hannah, both of whom are at first unable to conceive.

In his collection of modern midrashim for children of all ages, *Does God Have a Big Toe?*, Rabbi Marc Gellman suggests that the shofar was chosen, specifically, for several reasons: It is made from natural material; it is loud and can make beautiful sounds; and it is often challenging to produce those beautiful sounds. He writes that this is just like the challenge of beginning a new year and how difficult it is to give up bad habits, make good choices, forgive, and ask for forgiveness.

We also start the secular new year with noisemakers, but the noisemaker of Rosh Hashanah, the shofar, is our wake-up call, our reminder leading up to the High Holidays that we are being summoned to do the challenging work of true and honest introspection, that the time has come to ask ourselves the difficult questions, to look at our actions, commitments, and the relationships that we may not have attended to during the rest of the year.

It is the shrill sound of the shofar which is meant to awaken us to this task.

What have I been stubbornly refusing to face this past year which the shofar is calling me to face now?

How can I begin? What steps can I take to begin making change?

Day 21

21 Elul

שההינו

Shehecheyanu

Blessed are You, Eternal One, our God, Sovereign of the Universe, who has given us life, and has sustained us, and has enabled us to reach this moment.

The *Shehecheyanu* is recited after the blessing for the sounding of the shofar. We also recite it after lighting the candles at the beginning of Rosh Hashanah and of Yom Kippur. The Shehecheyanu dates back almost two thousand years and is found in the Talmud. It is customary to recite it to express gratitude for reaching a particular occasion. It is a part of the rituals for most holidays.

This blessing is recited when we perform a commandment for the first time in a new year, such as lighting the candles on the first night of Chanukah, dwelling in the sukkah, or eating matzah on Passover. It is traditionally recited when one does something for the first time or for the first time in a long time. Some Jews recite the Shehecheyanu the first time they eat a fruit which they have not eaten before. Some recite the Shehecheyanu on other happy firsts like earning a driver's license, traveling to Israel, or wearing a new outfit.

In this blessing, we acknowledge that there is a greater power beyond us and that we do not control everything. We express appreciation for the very fact that we have life, that we have been given the opportunity to live and breathe and to experience all that life has to offer, including this particular moment for which we are reciting the blessing. We are recognizing that the blessing is not just the life we have been given but all that has gone into maintaining it, all the nurturing and nurturers, ourselves included, who have allowed us to experience this with full awareness. And we are grateful for this particular moment in time.

This blessing reminds us to pause, to breathe, to recognize the moment as sacred. This blessing calls our attention to the sacredness of the moment and to express awe and gratitude for being alive to appreciate it. It reminds us to be present and not let the moment or its potential go unrecognized.

This is a powerful ritual that our ancestors incorporated into the cycle of our year and the cycle of our lives to remind us of the sacredness of a given moment.

How can I take greater note of the Shehecheyanu moments, both large and small, in my life?

How can I more regularly take time to recognize these moments with appreciation and gratitude?

Are there moments or times in my life longing to be recognized?

Day 22

22 Elul

ונתנה תקף קדשת היום

Unetaneh Tokef:
Let Us Proclaim the Holiness of this Day

Every person passes before You as a flock of sheep. Like a shepherd seeks out his flock, causing his flock to pass beneath his staff, so do You cause every living being to pass before You as You count and number every living being . . . and You inscribe their destiny.

The inspiration behind the writing of the *Unetaneh Tokef* is powerful and awe-inspiring. The traditional melody and words convey this. We are even told in this prayer that the angels are quaking in fear. Perhaps they are quaking on behalf of us, anxious about our fate, acting as our heavenly advocates and sympathizers.

According to the traditional story, Rabbi Amnon was being pressured to convert. As a way of evading an answer, he requested to be permitted to consider this for three days. At the end of the three days, failing to appear before the tyrants who put this question to him, he was arrested and was compelled to plead guilty. The punishment he received was that his hands and feet were cut off. Rabbi Amnon requested to be brought to the synagogue on Rosh Hashanah and there he recited the Unetaneh Tokef, a prayer which came to him by way of inspiration. He died immediately upon finishing the recitation. The story continues that three days later, Rabbi Amnon appeared to another great rabbi of the time and taught him the prayer so that it could be introduced to all synagogue communities.

This prayer presents one of many challenging images associated with Rosh Hashanah and Yom Kippur. When we confront these words, we are called to come face-to-face with our beliefs about God. Do I believe in a God who is omnipotent and numbers and determines the days of my life? How do I sort through my personal experiences with illness and death, with those I know whose lives were cut short prematurely or tragically? How do I square this with my hope or belief in a beneficent, compassionate God, the God who according to tradition visits Abraham as he is healing from his circumcision, the God who comforts the mourners?

This prayer calls upon the metaphor of God as shepherd. The shepherd looks after his or her sheep. Is this what I believe when I think about God? Is God my Comfort, my Rock? Is God determining my destiny?

What do I believe about God?

In what ways and at what moments do I feel God's presence in my life?

Do I find comfort when I feel God's presence?

Day 23

23 Elul

בראש השנה יכתבון

On Rosh Hashanah It Shall Be Inscribed

On Rosh Hashanah it shall be inscribed, and on Yom Kippur it shall be sealed. How many shall pass on and how many will be created; who shall live and who shall die . . . .

If we truly reflect on the words, it is difficult to recite them or to hear them chanted in the somber and almost foreboding melody without being overcome with thoughts: thoughts of those who prayed beside us last year who have since succumbed to illness or died unexpectedly; thoughts of who may no longer be with us next year at this time. We also think about those who have joined our families and our lives.

For those of us feeling the burden of aging or who are dealing with health issues, we may be wondering whether we may live to recite these words again next year. We are facing our mortality, and this prayer pulls no punches. It compels us to face subjects which we and our culture try so hard to avoid—death, dying, and mortality.

This prayer also challenges us with other questions. It asks: *Who shall be at peace, who shall be in comfort, who shall become rich, who shall be raised up?* And, while not asking it directly, it implies another question as well: *Who is responsible for these things?*

Can I have an impact on the answers to these questions? Who, if anyone, can do something to change the answers? Are the answers to the questions posed in this prayer beyond me or can I and those in my life alter those perhaps not so predetermined answers?

The verse that follows seems to suggest an answer:

And repentance, and prayer, and acts of righteousness can temper the severity of the decree.

What have I been doing or might I do to raise myself—to bring peace, to bring richness, to bring comfort of mind, body, and soul into my life?

What have I been doing or might I do to raise others—to bring peace, to bring richness, to bring comfort into their lives?

Is there someone in my life whom I am neglecting? What steps can I begin to take to remedy that?

Day 24

24 Elul

ותשובה

And Repentance

And repentance, and prayer, and acts of righteousness can temper the severity of the decree.

The tradition says that God is weighing our deeds in the Book of Life and determining whether we merit to be written in the Book of Life for another year. We are told in this prayer that we have the power to affect the outcome of that decree. The first thing we can do is to turn ourselves around. While *teshuvah* is often translated as "repentance," it may be more precisely understood as "returning" or "turning back." This helps to give us insight into what may be meant by the idea of repentance and how we might accomplish this.

The fact is that we pray all year for repentance, for the ability and strength to turn back, inward, to the way we know to be true and right. *Teshuvah* is a part of our daily liturgy; we pray for repentance three times a day in the weekday Amidah: *Praised are You, Eternal One, who welcomes repentance.* On these holy days, however, the stakes seem higher, the consequences a matter of life or death.

When we consider the idea of repentance or return, we can imagine ourselves on a path. The path is our life. Though we may still be seeking to understand what it all has meant, we know where we have been. We may even think we know where we are headed. Of course, there are surprises along the way. There are decisions and ethical dilemmas, as well as temptations which may lead us astray. The path we choose can change everything. I am reminded of the classic poem by Robert Frost, *The Road Not Taken.*

> *Two roads diverged in a wood, and I—*
> *I took the one less traveled by,*
> *And that has made all the difference.*

As we make choices in life about which road to take, we may think we know what lies ahead. While the ideal may be to make the best decisions we can with the information we have, the question remains, how do I return to the right path when I realize I have made a wrong turn?

What would repentance look like in my life?

In what ways have I been wandering on the wrong path?

How can I bring myself back to the right path?

What is the first step to *teshuvah,* to returning?

Day 25

25 Elul

ותפילה

And Prayer

And repentance, and prayer, and acts of righteousness can temper the severity of the decree.

The second way in which we are told we can impact our destiny is through prayer. *Tefillah*, the Hebrew word for prayer, is related to the reflexive form of the Hebrew, meaning "to judge." One goal of prayer, therefore, is to judge oneself and thereby, ideally, to transform oneself. This is a primary goal of the work of these holy days and the days which precede them. But, like repentance, it is part of daily Jewish life. Prayer is a daily, year-round experience.

There are many reasons why we pray. These are likely to be as diverse as the people who are praying. We pray because we are grateful, or feeling guilty, or in need. We pray when we are seeking solace and when we are in awe. Some pray because they believe it is commanded. Some pray to bring themselves closer to God. Often it is for a combination of reasons.

Prayer can and most certainly does look different for every person. Some choose to pray silently like Hannah, who we read of in the haftarah on the first day of Rosh Hashanah. Some prefer to be in a congregation, among community. Some prefer to be surrounded by nature. For some, it depends upon the moment and the need at any particular time.

For many of us, wearing special clothing or incorporating ritual objects helps us to pray with *kavannah* (intention). Many wear a *kippah*. On Shabbat and holidays, many adults over the age of Bar or Bat Mitzvah wear a *tallit;* and on weekdays, some wear *tefillin.* Some wear these for reasons of ritual, or because it is tradition. Others wear them because these ritual objects can help one feel more connected to the prayers and God. Some wear these ritual objects because they help one connect to past generations.

Prayer, of course, comes with challenges. If one prays at certain traditional times (Shabbat, holidays, daily), one may struggle to feel connected to the words of the prayers or the meaning behind them. The question becomes: Can prayer be a more meaningful part of my life, and can it transform me? What would that look like for me?

What role does prayer presently play in my life?

What challenges do I have with the idea of prayer?

How can prayer be a more a meaningful part of my life?

How would I like to see prayer transform me?

Day 26

26 Elul

וצדקה

And Acts of Righteousness

And repentance, and prayer, and acts of righteousness can temper the severity of the decree.

The third of the three ways we are told in this prayer that we can impact our fate is through acts of righteousness. The Hebrew word *tzedakah* is often said to mean "charity" but more accurately translates as "justice" or "righteousness." In Deuteronomy 16:20, we read: "Justice, justice you shall pursue." The Hebrew for the repeated word "justice" is *tzedek*.

Tzedakah is the giving of money and material goods to those in need. There is, in fact, a *mitzvah* (commandment) associated with most holidays that commands a particular act of righteousness. On Purim, we are commanded to give gifts to the poor in commemoration of one of the ways our ancestors celebrated their victory over the enemy. On Passover, we are commanded to help those in need to purchase Passover foods so that they, too, may observe the holiday. Our tradition teaches us that it is incumbent upon us to help those in need. These are *mitzvot*, commandments. We don't help others simply because it is nice or because it feels good, though this may be true. We give tzedakah because we are commanded to do so in the Torah, and we are told so repeatedly. Even those with little are commanded to help those who have even less.

Needless to say, there are many ways to give to others and there is no shortage of discussions about preferred ways of giving. Maimonides, the renowned medieval Torah commentator and physician, even developed an eight-rung "ladder" of tzedakah—from what he considered to be the lowest level of giving (giving unwillingly) to the highest (helping someone become self-sufficient). No matter how we give the fact remains that according to Jewish tradition and law, it is incumbent upon us to perform acts of right-eousness.

What role does *tzedakah* play in my life?

How would I like to see that change?

What are the obstacles to making that change?

What is the first step I can take to make that change?

Intermezzo

If you are following this text in order, then we are only a few days from Rosh Hashanah and with it, the sounding of the shofar, the sweet taste of apples dipped in honey, and the beginning of the Days of Awe, culminating in Yom Kippur, the Day of Atonement.

The previous three readings have each focused on a different aspect of the repeated refrain of the *Unetaneh Tokef* prayer. After the haunting reminder of what the future may hold and that this ultimately rests in God's hands, we are told that repentance, prayer, and acts of righteousness may temper the severity of the decree.

If you have read and journaled on these last pages, then you have been reflecting on the role these pillars of Judaism play in your life.

These next pages invite each of us to choose one or more of these three values to bring into our lives with more intention during the coming year. It may be an opportunity to extend something that we are already doing, to go a bit beyond our comfort zone, or to try something we have been wanting to try but have not yet done for one reason or another.

This may be an opportunity to bring something new into our lives or to repair something that has felt broken.

The following pages offer some ideas to consider as we each reflect on making a deeper commitment towards one or more of these values. Whatever you may decide, you are encouraged to make a commitment to something that feels manageable. If committing to a year is too daunting, begin with a month. If committing to a daily practice is too overwhelming, try a weekly action.

You may wish to use some of the journaling pages which follow this section to reflect on the impact of this new practice. You may choose to reflect on the challenges or obstacles to incorporating a new practice into your life. It is worth considering how your choice or decision has impacted others as well.

If you decide on a particular action which has not worked out for one reason or another, reflect on why and then try something else or some other version of your original choice.

Look upon this not only as an experiment but also as an opportunity to foster your personal growth as well as your relationship to these Jewish values.

Teshuvah
Repentance, Return

תשובה

The concept of repentance may feel abstract, and the work required, once it is determined, may feel emotionally overwhelming. The concept of turning back to the right path is so individual, for each of us is on a different journey. The suggestions below are ideas that can have the potential to provide balance, to bring our actions in line with our values, to repair and deepen our relationships, and to recalculate the course that we may be on but that we may feel has taken us astray.

Consider asking forgiveness of someone whom you feel you have wronged in some way.

Consider giving up (or taking steps to give up) a habit that you would like to break (e.g., smoking, over-eating, nail-biting, etc.).

Consider focusing on one area that you would like to change, that would lead you to feeling better about yourself and about how you live in the world. Perhaps choose something which would help remind you that you are made in God's image.

Consider your use of words in your daily life:

- Make a commitment to be more mindful of speaking of others when not in their presence.

- Make a commitment to be open and honest with people in your life when you feel hurt by them.

- Practice words of gratitude more regularly. Often we are appreciative of others or admire them for various reasons but do not take the time to let them know it.

- Make a time each day or each week to reach out to someone and let that person know how much he or she means to you.

- Send an email, make a call, or write a note to someone you have been thinking about just to let him or her know that. Make this a regular habit.

Tefillah
Prayer

תפילה

The concept of prayer can be challenging. We may struggle with the meaning of prayers, the relevance of some prayers, the idea that prayers often seem to go unanswered, and, of course, with our relationship with God, the One to whom we pray. Following are some ideas on committing to prayer or to the examination of the role of prayer in your life.

Consider setting aside a specific time of day, for even just a few minutes, to:

- Reflect on three things for which you are grateful (some use a gratitude journal).

- Meditate.

- Read an inspirational text or quotation. Journal about your thoughts on it.

Consider attending a morning or evening minyan at a local synagogue. Choose a day of the week and try to attend weekly for a month or more. (Your presence will also mean a lot to those reciting the Mourners' Kaddish.)

Consider attending a Shabbat evening or Shabbat morning service.

- If you live in an area where there are many prayer communities, visit one that is new to you once or twice a month on Shabbat. Bring your family or friends. You may discover a ritual, melody, prayer, or teaching which speaks to you. If you do, share that with others in your life.

- If you do not typically wear a tallit or put on tefillin or a kippah (or other headcovering), try it when you attend a prayer service. Afterwards, consider whether it brought greater meaning to the experience.

Consider bringing a prayerbook to a place you consider spiritual (e.g., the ocean, a lake, or a park) and reading some of the prayers in that setting. Reflect on whether the setting impacts the power of the prayers for you.

If *brachot* (blessings) are not part of your daily life, consider reciting blessings before and after eating or on other occasions. Our tradition has a blessing for just about everything.

Tzedakah
Acts of Righteousness

צדקה

It is difficult to argue with the idea of bringing more and greater righteousness into the world. We might, however, have different ideas about how to do this or how to do this in a more regular or meaningful way or perhaps how our actions can do the most good.

Consider recycling something which you don't regularly recycle. It may require a little research. It is only in the last few decades that paper, bottle, and can recycling have become a regular part of our culture and our habits. Batteries can be collected and disposed of more safely. Natural cork can be recycled and repurposed as can sport shoes. A little research can bring a new habit into your life and benefit the world around us. It can also reduce waste. Your example or newly gained knowledge can also influence the actions of others.

Consider setting aside an hour per month for your household to go through clothing, books, toys, etc. to donate to organizations and individuals in need. There are organizations which collect most anything you can imagine, from baby clothing to musical instruments to kitchen supplies.

Consider doing community service each month. By taking note of emails and notices in local newspapers, you may discover organizations and causes which speak to you. Bringing friends or family members can make it even more meaningful.

Consider carrying a tzedakah purse to more readily give to anyone in need. You may wish to commit to give a dollar to each person. If you prefer, give food or water instead of money. Consider trying this for a designated amount of time and reflect on the experience afterwards. You may be moved to continue.

Getting to know another person by name and sharing yours has the power to transform the interaction and bring greater meaning to the moment and to each of you. The next time you have a moment and give a dollar or food to someone in need, consider introducing yourself and politely asking his or her name.

Which of the three–*teshuvah*, *tefillah*, or *tzedakah*–are you going to explore further this year? How?

Once undertaken, reflect on the experience.

Day 27

27 Elul

זכרונותינו

Our Remembrances

May the offering of our lips be deserving of Your favor, most high and exalted God, who understands and hears our sounding of the shofar. Accept with compassion and desire our recital of the Remembrances.

Remembering is a theme that recurs in the Torah and is particularly present in our High Holiday liturgy. We repeatedly implore God to remember us—to remember us for a good life, for example. The *Yizkor* service on Yom Kippur is, of course, all about remembering those closest to us who are no longer living.

One of the sections of the Shofar service on Rosh Hashanah is *Zichronot*—Remembrances. It includes a number of instances in the Torah in which we read, *And God remembered . . . .*

God remembered Noah and his family on the ark during the time of the Flood. On Rosh Hashanah, we read the verses in Genesis in which it is written that God remembered Sarah who was, at the time, barren. In the Book of Exodus, God hears the moaning of the children of Israel enslaved in Egypt, and we are told then that God remembered the covenant God made with Abraham, Isaac, and Jacob.

The High Holidays are so intricately and intimately tied to our memories. For those who were raised Jewish, we recall childhood memories of the holy days—the foods, traditions, and, of course, the people.

Our memories can also call upon us to reflect on who we were at earlier times in our lives and who we have become. Who were the people who impacted us and contributed to who we have become? Did we and *do* we have Jewish role models who have inspired us in our relationship to religion? By the same token, were there aspects of those times which negatively impacted us and perhaps even drove us away from our relationship to our faith?

The holy days naturally bring us to reflect on the seminal moments and central people in our lives.

What would I like to hold onto and remember from this past year?

What are some of the significant and meaningful memories of the holidays from past years? How have they impacted me?

Are there traditions that I have let go of but that I would like to bring back into my life?

Who have been the models of faith in my life and how have they influenced me?

Day 28

28 Elul

ארשת שפתינו

May the Request of Our Lips Be Deserving of Your Favor

May the request of our lips be deserving of Your favor, most high and exalted God, who understands and hears our sounding of the shofar.

We ask that God hear our prayers and our requests, and we hope that this finds favor with God. We pray to God for many things and at many times. This may be especially true when we are praying on behalf of a loved one who is ill or at a time of crisis. We are grateful when God hears our prayers, and, for example, a loved one recovers from an illness. But how do we come to terms with the prayers that seem to go unanswered?

Are we putting God in a no-win situation when we pray, particularly when we pray for a miracle? What does it do to our faith when those prayers seem to fall on deaf ears? What does it mean if it appears that God answers some prayers and not others?

Should our prayers be phrased differently? Rabbi John Rosove of Temple Israel of Hollywood in Los Angeles teaches that rather than praying for the healing of a loved one, we should consider praying for everyone's strength and courage to deal with what may come. Rabbi Gary Oren of the American Jewish University prays for the wisdom of the healer and that he or she may get a good night's sleep and not get into an argument with his or her spouse before performing surgery. It may be a bit tongue-in-cheek, but it is also more about the realities of our world than about the vagaries of the world in which God resides.

Is it fair to bind our relationship with God to the outcome of a prayer? Perhaps we can consider what we are asking of God before we request that God hears our prayers and acts on them.

How do I see God's favor in my life other than when my prayers have been answered?

Aside from having my prayers answered, why else would I want my words to "win God's favor?"

For what do I pray to God?

How can I pray in a way that gives me some control and makes God a partner to whom I can speak?

Day 29

29 Elul

העבריינים

To Pray with Transgressors

By the authority of the heavenly court,
And by the authority of the earthly court;
With the consent of the Eternal One,
And with the consent of the congregation;
We declare it lawful to pray with transgressors.

In this introduction to the evening service of Yom Kippur and the preface to the *Kol Nidrei* prayer, we declare ourselves and those with whom we pray as transgressors, *ha'avaryanim*, those who have passed beyond what is ethical and moral.

This beginning to the holiest day of the Jewish year calls me to be unwaveringly honest with myself. I have transgressed. One hopes that I can say of myself and the others in the room that we have not murdered, that we have not raped, that we have not abused a child, that our transgressions are not so extreme. But we are also reminded that we cannot be so brazen, so out of touch as to declare that we have not crossed the line—intentionally or unintentionally, knowingly or unknowingly. In my heart of hearts, I know that even if I have, through my efforts, done better than last year, I still have a way to go.

As we read in the confessional prayers, many of the actions which have caused us to cross the line are not about heinous crimes such as murder and physical or sexual abuse. Many are about day-to-day behaviors such as how we treat parents and teachers, how we speak about others, and even how we eat and drink.

We are called to be honest about what is in the heart. We are called to reflect on the way we talk about others and the way we talk to others in our lives. Perhaps reciting these transgressions aloud allows us to take that first step toward acknowledging that we can each do better. Now that they are said aloud, floating in the room in a chorus of our voices, we can begin to think about how we can do better.

As we recite these words we have a choice: we can face up to these transgressions, own them, take responsibility for them. Or we can deny and avoid and make excuses. These words call upon each of us to admit and accept that we have transgressed. We have passed beyond what is ethical and moral. Saying this aloud may be the first step toward return and repentance.

Let me begin by opening my heart and considering the areas in which I have transgressed not only in my relationships, but in my professional life, the way that I walk in the world, and even against myself.

In my heart of hearts, what are my transgressions?

How do I come to terms with those transgressions that I am not yet prepared or willing to change?

Day 30

1 Tishrei

כל נדרי

Kol Nidrei: All Vows

All personal vows we are likely to make, all personal oaths and pledges we are likely to take between this Yom Kippur and the next Yom Kippur, we publicly renounce. Let them all be relinquished and abandoned, null and void, neither firm nor established. Let our personal vows, pledges, and oaths be considered neither vows nor pledges nor oaths.

This prayer in Aramaic lends its name to the evening service of Yom Kippur. It is more than a thousand years old. The focus is on vows we make to ourselves, and while it began as referring to annulling vows made in the past year, it was amended to refer to vows made for the upcoming year.

Historically, the Kol Nidrei prayer was used by those Jews at the time of the Spanish Inquisition who were forced to swear allegiance to another faith but, at the risk of their own lives, continued to practice Jewish rituals in private. The Kol Nidrei text was used as a way of annulling this vow made to the authorities.

The melody used in most Ashkenazic services was composed in the beginning of the sixteenth century. The prayer is chanted before sunset and is repeated three times, each time progressively louder and less hesitant, with greater strength and greater confidence.

We may reflect on the vows we have made to ourselves in the past year as well as on the vows we have made to others. It is an opportunity to reflect on whether we have made positive strides

toward following through on those vows or whether they were for-
gotten as the memory of Yom Kippur faded.

What vows have I made to myself in the past year?

How do I feel I have managed in the keeping of those vows?

What realistic vows will I make to myself and others in the coming year?

Day 31

2 Tishrei

אשמנו

Ashamnu: We Have Trespassed

We have trespassed; We have dealt treacherously;
We have robbed; We have spoken slander;
We have acted perversely; We have done wrong;
We have acted presumptuously; We have done violence;
We have practiced deceit; We have counseled evil;
We have spoken falsehood; We have scoffed;
We have revolted; We have blasphemed;
We have rebelled; We have committed iniquity;
We have transgressed; We have oppressed;
We have been stiff-necked; We have acted wickedly;
We have dealt corruptly; We have committed abomination;
We have gone astray; We have led others astray.

The *Ashamnu* is one of the most familiar liturgical pieces of the High Holiday prayers. An early form of this confessional prayer is found in Daniel 9:5–19. Within this biblical text, we read that the supplicant acknowledges himself or herself to be without merit and confesses to being guilty of transgressions. We pray that God will forgive based only on God's own merit.

We beat our chests as we recite the *Ashamnu*, an alphabetical acrostic of our shortcomings. The list is notable for several reasons. First, it is alphabetical—it seems an odd, almost poetic choice for a list of sins. One explanation for the form of this confessional is that it reminds us that the list of our faults is a long one, and, although it is finite, each transgression covers a large territory of behaviors. So, perhaps the format serves to remind us that our faults may be many, but they are ultimately finite in number.

The confessional is also in the plural like so much of the High Holiday liturgy. This may be so that we cannot exclude ourselves from culpability. Although I may not have committed a particular transgression, I can still understand each of these actions—literally or metaphorically—as ones which I have in some way been party to. Perhaps I have a responsibility because I stood idly by with knowledge of it or I have chosen ignorance while friends, community members, elected officials, or society has perpetuated these acts without even a word from me. Perhaps this prayer is written in the plural to acknowledge that we are all in this together, and separating oneself from the bad in the community is nonetheless still separating oneself from the community at large. We are reminded specifically in *Pirkei Avot* 2:5 (*Ethics of Our Ancestors*) *not* to separate ourselves from the community.

Perhaps this prayer is written in the plural for *all* the reasons above. But whichever reasons we believe, we beat our chests, we recite these words, and we try to understand the words in terms of our own lives. And rather than reciting each and following it with the thought of *Yes, that's me* or *No, that's not me*, perhaps the challenge is to ask: <u>How</u> *is that me?* <u>How</u> *am I responsible for this?*

Focusing on one or more of the transgressions included in the Ashamnu, how does this manifest itself in my life?

What might I do to correct this falling short, this missing of the mark?

How might I take action rather than stand idly by when I am aware of the perpetuation of one of these transgressions?

Day 32

3 Tishrei

עַל חֵטְא

Al Chet: For the Sin

Now may it be Your will, God of our ancestors, to forgive all of our sins, to pardon all of our iniquities, and to grant atonement for all of our transgressions.

In the introduction to the *Al Chet*, we encounter three different Hebrew words which refer to our shortcomings: *chet*, *avon*, and *pesha*. Each refers to a different type of transgression. These terms encompass those actions which are inadvertent and unintentional, those which result from temptation or a moment of weakness, and those which are deliberate and intentional.

The transgressions are many and even those committed against our fellow human beings are also committed against God. We harm God and God's world by hurting those with whom we share it. We recite this confessional prayer in the plural. And we are not excused for those instances when we missed the mark, however unintentionally. Whether accidentally or intentionally, whether in public or private, we are responsible for our behavior and for the consequences. This is our opportunity to own up to and take responsibility for that behavior and the harm it has caused, might have caused, or may cause in the future. By doing so, we take the first step toward healing our relationships and our own self. In this way, we can begin the difficult task of self-transformation.

In this confessional, we ask God to forgive us and grant us atonement. One of the predominant themes of this holiday season is that of forgiveness. For some, it is traditional to ask forgiveness of everyone in their lives. They may say: If I have done anything which has hurt you, I hope you will forgive me. We recognize that there are times when we may unintentionally hurt someone. We may not realize that we have used words which hit a tender emotional spot.

We are called upon, challenged to look deep within ourselves and to acknowledge the harm to which we have been party, the damage we have done to ourselves and to others and to ask forgiveness. If we have in some way hurt another, we must ask forgiveness of that person. Only then can we approach God to forgive us as well. So, we are challenged to put ego and blame aside and seek forgiveness from others as well as to forgive ourselves.

Seeking forgiveness can be difficult but is a part of our daily lives. Perhaps this is why it is found in the weekday Amidah throughout the year when we pray: *Forgive us for we have sinned.* The challenge is to ask forgiveness from those we have wronged and to accept the sincere apologies of those who have wronged us. Perhaps this prayer, in asking God to forgive, is reminding us that we are each called to do the same.

From whom or for what do I need to ask forgiveness?

What will make this difficult? How can I take the first step?

Has someone requested my forgiveness? Is there something which makes forgiving challenging for me?

Day 33

4 Tishrei

כי אנו אמך

We Are Your People

We are Your people, and You are our God.
We are Your children, and You are our Parent.
We are Your servants, and You are our Eternal One.
We are Your community, and You are our Heritage.

In this selection, we reflect on our relationship with God and the myriad ways in which it manifests. God is my parent, my creator, my shepherd, my beloved, my friend. I am God's chosen one, God's sheep, God's follower, God's child.

One's relationship with God is multi-faceted and, for many of us, ever-changing. We refer to God in different ways, at different times, calling upon different aspects of our relationship with God. At times, we are God's partner, and at other times, God's servant. We see these references in the text and liturgy as well as in Midrash.

In the beginning of the Amidah, recited three times daily all year, we repeat the word *Elohei* before the name of each of our ancestors.[2] One might ask, why not just say, *The God of Abraham, Isaac, and Jacob* rather than *The God of Abraham, the God of Isaac, and the God of Jacob?* We are, after all, referring to the same God. One commentary explains that while they each prayed to the same God, each had a unique relationship with God. In that same way, each of us has a unique relationship with God. By extension,

---

[2] In many communities, this includes the matriarchs as well.

we can also understand that at different times in our lives, we may each relate differently to God. At certain times, we stand before God as a child does before a parent. At other times, as a partner, and at still other times, as one who seeks to serve. Our relationship with God is complex and no doubt impacted by the circumstances of our lives.

On the High Holidays, the images are more about God as Sovereign and as Judge. God has the power. But we also imagine God as merciful, as compassionate and loving and having mercy upon us as God considers our transgressions.

This prayer seems in some way to be a reminder to God to have mercy on each of us at this awe-filled moment. Remember that You are my merciful parent; remember that You created me. Remember that You are my shepherd. I am in your care.

How do I best understand my relationship with God?

When is this relationship most secure and when is it most tenuous?

What do I expect from God?

What can God expect from me?

Day 34

5 Tishrei

וסמך אהרון את שתי ידו

And Aaron Shall Place Both of His Hands

And Aaron shall place both of his hands upon the head of the live goat, and confess over him all the iniquities of the children of Israel, and all their transgressions, even all their sins; and he shall put them upon the head of the goat, and shall send him away into the wilderness by the hand of an appointed man.

The Torah reading for Yom Kippur morning is from the portion *Acharei Mot,* found in Leviticus 16. It is followed by the *maftir aliyah* (an additional aliyah) from Numbers 29:7–11, which describes the Yom Kippur sacrifices.

The traditional Torah reading itself focuses on the rituals of Aaron and the ancient priests regarding the sin-offerings and the purpose of the atonement of the sins of the priests and the people of Israel. It includes the ritual of symbolically placing the transgressions of the people onto a goat (the original scapegoat) and sending it into the wilderness. The reading also includes the commandment to observe the tenth day of the seventh month as a day of atonement (*Yom haKippurim*), a day of abstinence from daily activities and of complete rest.

Yom Kippur is the Sabbath of Sabbaths, the holiest day of the Jewish year. The Torah recounts in this reading, as well as in others, a detailed process for the atonement of sins. While there is a public confessional which is part of the liturgy, there must also be a personal confession, when we say aloud to ourselves that which we must do to bring ourselves closer to the person we hope to be.

We reflect on what it will take to bring our actions in line with the values by which we aspire to live.

We may ask: What is it that I must do in order to be the person that I imagine that God would want me to be? When I look in the mirror, can I feel that I am truly in God's image, that I see the divine spark in myself?

Are there rituals that have become part of my life that help me to be the person I want to be? What are those rituals?

Are there rituals I can add to my life that might help me move toward this goal? What are those rituals?

Day 35

6 Tishrei

הלוא זה צום אבחרהו

Behold, This Is the Fast I Am Seeking

Behold! This is the fast day which is precious to me.
Loosen the chains of wickedness, undo the bonds of oppression . . .
Share your food with the hungry, take the poor to your home,
Clothe the naked when you see them, never turn from your fellow
human being.

The haftarah that is traditionally read on Yom Kippur morning is taken from the writings of the prophet Isaiah. The people have complained that their fasts have not brought them the desired results. The response from God through the prophet is that God does not desire a fast for the sake of fasting and receiving atonement: "This is not the fast that the Eternal One asks of the people." God does not desire a fast day on which the people abstain from eating, sitting in sackcloth and ashes. God is asking us for a different kind of fast, a fast which is about the welfare of our fellow human beings, that we make a sacrifice on their behalf.

Isaiah continues God's message by encouraging the people to observe the Sabbath and find in it joy. That, he says, will lead one to find delight in God's goodness.

It is ironic—or perhaps crucial—that on this day of fasting we are reminded that fasting in and of itself does not serve the higher purpose. We fast to move ourselves to a higher purpose, to change our ways, and to bring ourselves and the world to a higher plane.

This physical self-denial is meant to lead us to pursue justice and kindness. It is a self-denial in which we give of our time and of our resources toward the goal of bringing wholeness, *shalom*, to the world. It is one in which we bring the beauty of the Sabbath and the holy days into our lives. These, in turn, according to the prophet, also bring us closer to God and to what God hopes for us.

By the same token, Yom Kippur is not a one day goal in and of itself. If we beat our chests on Yom Kippur for speaking poorly of others and return to this practice days later, we have not engaged in the true meaning of Yom Kippur in the way it was meant, and we have not taken full advantage of Yom Kippur to lift our souls and our lives and the lives of those with whom we share the world.

What actions do I take in the world which represent the fast that Isaiah says that God truly desires?

What would I like to do which I have not yet done?

What obstacles stand in the way of reaching this goal?

What steps can I take toward making this change and removing these obstacles?

Day 36

7 Tishrei

יזכור

Yizkor: May God Remember

May God remember the soul of____, who has passed on to his/her eternal rest. I pledge acts of righteousness on his/her behalf and pray that his/her soul be kept among the souls of Abraham, Isaac, and Jacob, Sarah, Rebecca, Rachel, and Leah, and all the righteous in Gan Eden. Amen.

The *Yizkor* service is one of the centerpieces and, for many, one of the central associations of Yom Kippur. It is a service in which we remember those in our lives who no longer are part of the physical world but who hold a place in our hearts. It is about the power of memory and the importance of remembering. It is a time in which we recall their names and our relationship with them.

While most are familiar with the Yizkor of Yom Kippur, we also recite Yizkor on Shemini Atzeret[3] and during Passover and Shavuot.

Particularly fresh in our minds may be those in our lives with whom we observed these holidays last year but who have since died. The first year without a loved one, including all of the traditional times one might join together, such as holidays, birthdays, anniversaries, and other life-cycle events, is especially difficult because their absence may be particularly evident and leave a painful, gaping hole.

As a time for remembering loved ones who are no longer living, Yizkor can also bring up a host of conflicted feelings. There

---

[3] The day after the seventh day of Sukkot

are those among the dead with whom we, the living, have unresolved issues. There may be conversations never finished or never
even begun. Not all relationships are good or easy, even with those
closest to us: indeed, sometimes especially with those closest to us.
Some are filled with conflict, anger, or even abuse. Frequently,
death complicates the matter by giving permanence and finality to
an already challenging relationship. For this reason, the Yizkor service may be an especially difficult time.

One traditional understanding about why we say Yizkor on
Yom Kippur is that according to the *Zohar*, the foundational text of
Jewish mysticism, one who is affected to tears by the death of the
righteous will be forgiven, thus the connection between Yom Kippur
and Yizkor. Perhaps at this most tenuous time, during this prayer
service when we are moved to think about the most challenging
questions in our lives, we are in some way hoping that the merits of
those who have died will be considered as having a positive influence on our fate.

It is a tradition to give tzedakah in memory of a loved one
who has died. By the same token it is traditional to continue good
works in their memory. One might give tzedakah to a cause that
was important to him or her, educate others about a cause that he
or she held dear, or perhaps volunteer for an organization that
represents those values. And when we do any of the above, we can
remind ourselves that we are doing so in his or her name.

As I think about Yizkor this year, who is especially on my mind?

What do I miss about him or her?

How did he or she impact my life?

What might I commit myself to do in his or her memory?

As I reflect on those who have died, what unresolved issues are still present for me?

Day 37

8 Tishrei

אל-תטמאו

Do Not Defile Yourselves

And the Eternal One spoke to Moses, saying: Speak to the children of Israel, and say to them: I am the Eternal One, your God. After the doings of the land of Egypt, where you dwelled, you shall not do; and after the doings of the land of Canaan, to where I bring you, you shall not do; neither shall you follow their statutes. My ordinances you shall do, and My statutes you shall keep, to walk therein: I am the Eternal One, your God. You shall therefore keep My statutes, and My ordinances, which if a man obeys, he shall live: I am the Eternal One.

The traditional Torah reading for *mincha*, the afternoon service, of Yom Kippur is taken from Leviticus 18. The focus is on a description of forbidden marriages and relationships. According to one interpretation, this is to remind us, in the midst of asking forgiveness for our transgressions, not to lose our self-control and not to be tempted into forbidden relationships. Of course, what constitutes a forbidden relationship continues to change over time and varies among communities.

In some communities, alternative Torah passages are read such as from Leviticus 19, the holiness code, which has been adopted by the Reform movement as the Yom Kippur Torah reading at the mincha service.

If we examine some of the thematic threads that run between these readings, we read of the centrality of relationships— our relationship with God, with ourselves, and with one another.

While there are those in the world who prefer to be on their own and limit their interactions with others, for most of us, our relationships with others are central to the meaning and purpose of our lives. We often define ourselves and our identity by those relationships. In our relationships, there is the potential, and perhaps the ideal, to achieve a sense of sacredness or holiness. We can feel hurt or disappointed by others who are important to us and, in fact, often feel most hurt or disappointed by those who are the dearest to us or with whom we feel the closest.

Perhaps this reading on Yom Kippur is to serve as a reminder about how we treat one another and to what we should aspire in our relationships.

How do I recognize the sacredness of my relationships?

How do I treat those in my life as holy, as created by God and in God's image?

Is there anything I want or need to change in my relationships to reflect their sacredness? How can I move in that direction?

Which relationships in my life would I like to repair and how might I take that step?

Day 38

9 Tishrei

יונה

Jonah

And the word of the Eternal One came to Jonah, the son of Amittai, saying: "Arise, go to Nineveh, that great city, and proclaim against it; for their wickedness has come before Me."

The traditional *haftarah* reading for Yom Kippur afternoon is the Book of Jonah. It is found in the Book of Prophets, and we read the entire book of Jonah which is comprised of four chapters. By the end of the narrative, Jonah, the reluctant prophet, brings God's message to the people of Nineveh, and they repent their evil ways.

There are several traditional explanations for why the Book of Jonah is chanted on Yom Kippur. In the text, we read that God shows mercy for the sinners of the city of Nineveh. In other words, if God has mercy on them, then why would God not have mercy on us? A second explanation is that of repentance. The people of Nineveh seem to repent with great sincerity. They are role models for the power of sincere repentance. Third, we are reminded throughout the story that the earth and everything in it is in God's dominion and under God's control.

Finally, mincha is understood to be a particularly ripe time for prayers to be answered. Perhaps this lies in the liminal nature of the service, as the day is closing, the sun is beginning to set, and the evening is upon us. It is a time that holds the place between day and night, between light and dark, and perhaps symbolically between life and death. At this time during the long stretch of Yom Kippur when many may be at their hungriest and most vulnerable, we are reminded that just as Jonah and the people of Nineveh are saved from their fate, so we can be too.

Not only do we read of the repentance of the people of Nineveh, but in the final chapter, we read that God teaches Jonah that God's compassion extends to all God's creations. Perhaps just as God has compassion for the wicked people of Nineveh, God will have compassion for us and we will be forgiven. Perhaps there is, in this narrative, a sense of hope for each of us to turn back towards the right path. Perhaps we also learn that God's compassion extends to all of God's creations, and this may serve as a model to which we can aspire.

In one of the blessings traditionally recited following the haftarah, we ask for compassion from God. Shall we ask for compassion and at the same time not share it with others? Perhaps this is the lesson of the Book of Jonah.

Are there times when I feel short of compassion? If so, when are those times? Do I feel this way with certain people or around particular global concerns?

What are the obstacles I face toward bringing compassion into my life?

Do obstacles such as judgment, denial, or emotional disconnectedness get in the way?

How might I bring greater compassion for others into my life? Where can I begin?

Day 39

10 Tishrei

לא החזיק לעד אפו

God Does Not Retain Anger Forever

Who is a God like You, that pardons the iniquity, and passes by the transgression of the remnant of God's heritage? God does not retain anger forever, because God delights in mercy. God will again have compassion upon us; God will subdue our iniquities; and You will cast all their sins into the depths of the sea. You will show faithfulness to Jacob, mercy to Abraham, as You have sworn unto our ancestors from the days of old.

The haftarah for the mincha service of Yom Kippur, which begins with the reading of Jonah, ends with the above verses from the prophet Micah (7:18–20). In his words, we read of a compassionate God who is forgiving and merciful, who shows kindness and mercy to our ancestors and, we assume or hope with all of our heart, will show kindness and mercy to us. This God does not hold on to anger but instead is merciful and kind and casts away our sins.

While the God of the Torah is not always portrayed in a loving and forgiving light, here we read of a God with whom we can not only get on board but whom we can also strive to emulate.

In the *Gevurot* section of the Amidah, which we traditionally recite three times daily, we read of the God who is the healer of the sick, redeemer of the captive, and the one who lifts up the fallen. In Torah, we read of the God who clothes Adam and Eve, who visits Abraham after his circumcision, and who buries Moses at the end of his life. This is a forgiving, compassionate, and loving God. This is also a God who is acting in ways which we are encouraged to

167

emulate, for we are created in God's image according to the passage in Genesis. We are encouraged, therefore, to bring healing to those who are ill, to not sit idly by as the captive suffers, to clothe the naked, and to be present to help bury our dead and comfort the mourners.

In this passage from Micah, perhaps God is acting as a role model, teaching us to not hold on to anger. So many of us hold on to anger at those who hurt us intentionally or otherwise. This anger often creates an emotional if not a physical knot within us. This knot may prevent us from moving on with our lives or from healing otherwise meaningful and loving relationships. Perhaps in this short passage, we are being reminded that, like Micah's God, we are to show mercy, to delight in kindness, to give the benefit of the doubt, and to try to cast off our anger.

How does anger over past wounds fester and cause me pain?

Is there a wound or a rift that I can take a step towards healing?

How might I begin that process?

Day 40

11 Tishrei

שמע ישראל

Hear, O Israel

Hear, O Israel, Adonai is our God, Adonai is One.

These words are chanted aloud at the end of the Yom Kippur *Neilah* service and here mark the first day following Yom Kippur. The Shema becomes our transition from Elul and the Ten Days of Awe back into our daily lives.

The *Shema* is considered by many to be the most important prayer in the Jewish religion. It is traditionally recited as part of the *shacharit* (morning) and *ma'ariv* (evening) prayer services every day of the year, as well as before going to sleep. It is also traditionally recited by a person who is dying as a last testament of faith.

The Shema is found in the Torah, in the Book of Deuteronomy (6:4). When we recite the Shema, it is traditional to cover our eyes. We are testifying to God's oneness, and we are attempting to block out distractions, so that we may focus on the words and their meaning.

This prayer calls upon us to truly hear the words being spoken in our lives. We are called upon to hear the words of the others who are in our presence during our day-to-day lives and the others in the world. How often do we truly listen? We are on the phone with someone, perhaps multi-tasking. We are listening to a friend, and our minds are distracted, or perhaps we are thinking about how we may want to respond, just waiting for our friend to offer a pause so that we can say what is on our minds. How often do we respond to someone before he or she is finished speaking, perhaps even incorrectly assuming what it is that he or she intends to say?

This prayer reminds us of the power of listening and *truly* hearing the other—the friend, the family member, the person who we may not know but whose needs we also cannot and should not ignore. It is the final prayer of Yom Kippur and traditionally the final prayer of our life. It is a reminder of our mortality and also of our humanity.

In some communities, we stand as we recite the Shema—we are testifying to God's singularity in a metaphoric courtroom, and we are standing again at Mount Sinai. We are reminding ourselves of the power of recognizing God's presence in the world, of truly hearing God's voice; and, in turn, listening to the words of those with whom we share this world.

How can I be a better listener in my life?

What can I do to truly hear the voice of the other?

How can I listen to my own inner voice with greater care and attention?

How can I hear God's voice in my life with greater clarity?

שהחינו

Shehecheyanu

Blessed are You, Eternal One our God, Sovereign of the Universe, who has given us life, and has sustained us, and has enabled us to reach this moment.

We take a moment to celebrate the journey that we have each taken from the spiritual preparation of the month of Elul through the Ten Days of Awe.

I take a moment to express gratitude for the strength to look into myself, into my soul and to do the challenging yet rewarding work of *cheshbon hanefesh*, taking an accounting of my soul.

I take stock of the journey and look ahead to the challenge and the reward of continuing that journey and taking its riches and its future possibilities into the year ahead.

Blessed are You, Eternal One, for bringing me to this moment and for accompanying me and for giving me strength along this journey.

Continuing the Journey

As many of us know, the challenge of doing the work of introspection and self-reflection (and the commitments we make as a result) continues as we return to our daily lives from the sacred time we set aside during the holy days. The following section provides an opportunity for monthly check-ins to continue this work throughout the year.

You may choose to continue on your own, setting aside a regular time each month or as often as you like. You may choose to continue with others who have taken a similar journey and are looking for the support of a community of fellow "travelers" to continue those efforts.

For some, *Rosh Chodesh*, the first day of a new month in the Hebrew calendar, is a natural time to reflect. However you choose to continue the work, I encourage you to set aside some time regularly to continue to invest in the efforts you have already made.

October
Tishrei–Cheshvan

תשרי-חשון

We leave the somber reflective time of Yom Kippur, and, according to many, we go directly into the fulfillment of the next *mitzvah*, the constructing of the *sukkah,* central to the observance of the holiday of *Sukkot,* one of the three Pilgrimage festivals.

Sukkot begins five days after Yom Kippur at the full moon. We are commanded to dwell in the sukkah and to take the four species, represented by the *lulav* and *etrog.* We are not told why we take up the four species, though we are told to rejoice before God (Leviticus 23:40). We read in the Torah that we dwell in the sukkah to remember that God made our ancestors, the Israelites, live in booths when God brought us out of the Land of Egypt (Leviticus 23:43).

The seventh day of Sukkot is *Hoshanah Rabbah* and the following day is *Shemini Atzeret* (the Eighth Day of Assembly). The day after Shemini Atzeret is *Simchat Torah*. In Israel and in the Reform and Reconstructionist communities, these two holidays are combined together into one day.

One might think of Sukkot (referred to as *Z'man Simchateinu,* "season of our joy") as an opportunity to celebrate with family and friends, as we move from the solemnity of Yom Kippur. It is a time to join with loved ones, fulfill the commandment of welcoming others into one's sukkah, celebrate the season, and hope that we have each been written in the Book of Life for another year.

Sukkot is also a reminder of the fragility of our lives. We dwell in a temporary shelter which finds us vulnerable to the elements. We are reminded that we are intimately connected with nature as we look up and see the stars, the moon, and the sun through the roof. We feel the drops of rain as we sit around the table. We have just concluded the holy day of Yom Kippur during which we are, in essence, feeling our most vulnerable, as we pray for our very lives; and then we sit in a fragile hut, continuing to feel our vulnerability, reminded of our dependence on others and on forces more powerful than ourselves.

We are also reminded that we bring beauty into our lives, not through the material but through those things which, as the credit card commercial reminds us, are priceless. We decorate the sukkah and we dwell essentially in poverty. Our sukkot are minimalist— temporary walls, fragile roof, table, chairs, and decorations. We are reminded of the importance of relationships as we sit around the table with our guests. Our guests are the people sitting among us as well as the spiritual ancestors we invite in (*ushpizin*) and those who we wish could be with us but for one reason or another are not. But as with *Yizkor*, which we again recite on Shemini Atzeret, their impact on our lives can also fill the sukkah.

It is a joyous holiday, but the themes of the Ten Days of Awe continue to resonate when we allow them in.

How do I balance my acknowledgement of the fragility of life with my joy of living?

When I visualize dwelling in a sukkah, by whose presence do I wish to be surrounded and embraced?

November
Cheshvan–Kislev

חשון-כסלו

By the end of September, our thoughts are turning to autumn. In October and November, we are surrounded by the vibrant colors of the season. Depending on where one lives, the leaves on the trees may be turning various shades of orange, red, and yellow as they shed from the trees. But as the autumn air fills our daily lives, we begin looking toward the upcoming national holidays.

Thanksgiving is a holiday which in some ways binds most Americans. Many nations celebrate a day of giving thanks. In the Untied States, it is a holiday like few others, a day on which we can be reasonably sure that most Americans are enjoying a holiday meal. Some may be with friends or with family. Others who are less fortunate may be enjoying the traditional foods at a meal served at a church, synagogue, or shelter. While most of those dinners likely include the mainstays, families of different ethnic groups often add a few touches particular to their upbringing (perhaps matzah ball soup at a Jewish Thanksgiving dinner, for example).

According to some, Thanksgiving traces its roots to Sukkot, the Pilgrims having been a religious community which held the Bible close. Prior to 1789, there were various nods to the idea of a day of thanksgiving. In 1789, though, George Washington proclaimed the first national celebration of a day of giving thanks. The focus of that first Thanksgiving was to express our gratitude for the end of the War of Independence and the ratification of the United States Constitution. It was not, however, until Abraham Lincoln declared a national day of Thanksgiving in 1863 that it became an annual holiday.

While Thanksgiving is a day set in our calendars to be grateful, the Jewish tradition provides daily opportunities to take into account all for which we can be grateful. Built into the daily prayers are reminders to be grateful for the gift of our soul and our physical body, for creation, and for all that God has done for us throughout Jewish history. We are reminded in the daily Amidah to be grateful for all that we have in our lives and for life itself.

How else can we incorporate gratitude into our lives? Some use a gratitude journal. My friend and teacher, Monsignor Robert McNamara, once taught from his pulpit at an interfaith Thanksgiving celebration that we should thank God for three things every night before we go to sleep. When we think about this, it is not a difficult task to think of three things for which to be grateful—perhaps they are the things so many take for granted: food, shelter, health, family, a job, friends, or respect.

The second part of being thankful is verbalizing this to the people in our lives. It is a powerful moment when we take the time to express gratitude to another for something that may be understood or perhaps has remained unspoken. It is also a way in which we can continue the act of *teshuvah*, turning back. By taking note of and expressing our gratitude to God, to the universe, and to those in our lives, we see the possibility of transformation.

How do I practice gratitude in my life?

How can I make expressing gratitude a part of my daily life?

December
Kislev–Tevet

כסלו-טבת

The holidays of December, both Jewish and non-Jewish, share themes of light and darkness. At the darkest time of year, we light candles in observance of Chanukah. We add a new candle each night, bringing an increasing amount of light into our lives as the holiday progresses. Light also plays a dominant role in the observance of Christmas and Kwanzaa.

Among the schools of the great rabbis Hillel and Shammai (who often found themselves in disagreement), there were opposing opinions about the observance of the candle lighting.

The House of Shammai argued that we should light eight candles on the first night and one less on each successive night, because in the Chanukah story the amount of oil decreased each day. Therefore, each night we too should decrease our light.

The House of Hillel argued that we should increase our joy each day rather than decrease it, and therefore we should light an additional candle each night. As with most of their debates, the House of Hillel won out.[4]

As we enter this dark, cold time in the year, we are called to think about how we can bring greater light into the world, into our relationships, and into our own lives. We can reflect on the commitments we made to ourselves several months ago as our thoughts were so directed by the liturgy and the sermons of the High Holidays toward our introspection.

---

[4] I know at least one person who lights two Chanukah menorahs, one honoring each of these traditions, a beautiful way to keep alive Shammai's dissenting opinion.

The Hebrew word *Chanukah* is translated as "dedication." In the historical account of the holiday, it referred to the re-dedication of the Holy Temple in Jerusalem after it was desecrated by the Syrian-Greeks. But we can also imagine the need at the time—and for all time—to re-dedicate ourselves to striving to live a more pure and ethical life, one in which we bring ourselves closer to God and to the person we each know that we can be.

How can I bring greater light into my life, my relationships, and the world?

What might it mean to bring more light into my own life?

What can I do to rededicate myself to the goals I set forth in Elul and Tishrei?

January
Tevet–Shevat

טבת-שבט

The birthday of Martin Luther King, Jr. falls in mid-January. It is incredible to note that for many of us, in our lifetimes, the United States was not a nation that practiced liberty and justice for all. In some parts of the country, people were separated by race, and laws not only did not protect, but in some cases were outright discriminatory. They were designed to keep people separate and unequal.

We live in a nation which continues to struggle with the concept of liberty and justice for all. In some cases, laws are still discriminatory. As of this writing, there are many states in the United States in which one can be legally fired from a job simply because of one's sexual orientation. Those in the LGBT community are just now realizing equality in their marriages, finally able to claim all the rights of opposite-sex married couples.

We also live in a nation where many people of color feel oppressed, and, according to statistics, some groups are disproportionately imprisoned. In addition, there is a poverty of resources in many minority communities.

Rabbi Abraham Joshua Heschel, who marched with Dr. Martin Luther King, Jr., spoke of praying with our feet. Yes, we pray silently and in community, but we have the obligation to pray with our feet as well, to take action. No one of us is free until each one of us is free. If our neighbor does not have the benefit of all the rights of which I benefit, then I have a responsibility to act. I have the obligation to use my voice, my vote, my time, and my resources to stand beside my neighbor, just as he or she is obligated to stand up for me.

In the Book of Genesis, after Cain kills Abel and God asks, "Where is your brother?" Cain answers, "Am I my brother's keeper?" And God responds, "The voice of your brother's blood screams to me from the ground." (Genesis 4:9–10)

Yes, without question, we are each our brother's keeper and we are one another's brother and sister. This is one of the reasons we are told by our tradition that we can each trace our ancestry back to Adam and Eve. We are all connected and we are each responsible for one another.

As we consider the message of Martin Luther King, Jr., of Abraham Joshua Heschel, and of the text from Genesis, we are reminded of the call of the shofar; the call for repentance, prayer, and acts of righteousness.

In what ways do I put up walls, isolating myself from others with whom I share my world?

In what ways do I reach beyond those walls to truly get to know "the other?"

What might I do to "pray with my feet" on behalf of others?

February
Shevat–Adar I

שבט-אדר א

The holiday of *Tu b'Shevat*, commonly thought of as the new year of the trees, is observed on the 15th day of Shevat, which is the origin of its name. The holiday generally falls between mid-January and mid-February. It is one of four different new years which are part of the Jewish tradition, and it has become a day of acknowledging our relationship to nature and our appreciation of it. Customs include spending the day outdoors, planting trees (or donating to the planting of trees, particularly in Israel through the Jewish National Fund), and enjoying the fruit of the trees.

One custom which is actually several centuries old is that of the Tu b'Shevat seder. There are many variations of the Tu b'Shevat seder, though most of the *haggadot* which have been created borrow from the features of the Passover seder, such as the use of four cups of wine or grape juice. There are variations of this seder which are more kabbalistic in nature and others which are more focused on Israel and the seven species of the Holy Land that are mentioned in the Bible.

In some Tu b'Shevat seders, the four cups of wine or grape juice vary by color. We begin with a glass of white grape juice and then increasingly mix in the red grape juice until the final cup which is completely red. This is meant to symbolize the move from the barrenness of winter to the blossoming of spring.

Depending upon where one lives, this may still feel like a very cold, dark time of year, when nesting and cocooning feels more desirable than being outdoors. But this holiday calls us to begin considering the approaching spring.

Tu b'Shevat also calls upon us to reconsider our obligation to the world and to the Land of Israel by planting trees for example. We are called on to remind ourselves of our inextricable relationship with the natural world and our responsibility for it.

In the mystical tradition from which the Tu b'Shevat seder originates, the emphasis is on the symbolic nature of different types of fruits and nuts and accompanies the eating of these different species with spiritual readings. The focus becomes moving to increasingly greater spiritual planes and becoming closer and closer to God.

As I think back on the High Holidays, in what ways am I trying to deepen my connection to God and to those values and actions which I believe to be reflective of God's image?

How can I strive to deepen this goal? Through repentance? Through prayer? Through acts of righteousness?

How might I recommit myself to the natural world around me and to the Land of Israel?

March
Adar I–Adar II–Nisan

אדר א-אדר ב-ניסן

When we say that the holidays are early or late, it is, of course, not true, at least according to the Hebrew calendar. They always arrive on the same Hebrew date each year. It is where they fall on the Gregorian calendar that makes it appear as if they are early or late.

Because of how the Jewish calendar works, Passover may begin anytime from March to late April, just as Chanukah may arrive anytime from the cusp of Thanksgiving to the secular new year. The Jewish calendar operates on a nineteen year cycle, and specific years during that cycle are designated as leap years, during which an extra month is added to the calendar. This allows for the holidays to remain in the seasons to which they are intrinsically connected. The leap year in Hebrew is referred to as *shanah m'uberet*, a pregnant year. That extra month usually falls in March–April and is named Adar II or Adar Bet.

Typically, sometime between the end of February and mid-March, we celebrate Purim, which occurs in Adar II during a leap year in the Jewish calendar. At the heart of Purim is the question of identity. Esther hides who she is through most of the narrative. Her actions call on each of us to ask questions about how we embrace or struggle with aspects of our own identity. Do I choose to stand proudly and honestly for who I am and what I believe, or do I remain "in a closet" (sometimes of my own making)? Of course, there are countries and times in history as well as circumstances when it would not be wise to be open about who we are. Fortunately, that is certainly less the case now in much of the first world in the twenty-first century.

197

We can continue to reflect on the commitments we made during the High Holidays, and we can ask ourselves whether we are being authentic in our lives. Do we make choices that reflect our values and beliefs? In our relationships, do we choose to be honest about who we are or do we hide out of shame or fear? Are we honest about our feelings or do we find convenient excuses to avoid being authentic? Do we drape ourselves in "costumes" as a way of pretending to be what we are not and avoid being honest about who we are?

In what ways have I tried to be more authentic and honest with myself and with others?

In what ways have I continued to "dress up" and have not allowed others to know the true me?

What fears or obstacles prevent me from being more authentic in my life and relationships?

If I could choose one area or relationship in which to move toward greater authenticity, which would it be? What is my first step toward that end?

April
Adar II–Nisan–Iyar

אדר ב-ניסן-אייר

Passover falls in the middle of the month of Nisan, which is actually the first month of the Hebrew calendar, although we consider the new year to begin at Rosh Hashanah. Nisan, marks the commemoration of the Exodus from Egypt, the beginning of the journey of our people from slavery to liberation. Though it is our redemption, it is just the beginning of the journey.

The rituals of Passover are intended to connect us to the lives of our ancestors, the sensory memories of being enslaved and then being redeemed by God. We are meant to experience the harsh realities of the slavery (bitter herbs and salt water) and the joy of liberation (reclining and drinking sweet wine). The *charoset* is both of these rolled into one—the sweetness of freedom and the texture and color of the mortar our ancestors were forced to use in their back-breaking labor. In fact many of the rituals of Passover are simultaneously symbolic of slavery and redemption. Another example is the salt water which can be understood to be the tears of the slaves and is also understood by some to be like amniotic fluid, the birthing of a free people.

When we traditionally clear our homes of *chametz* prior to Passover, we are symbolically removing what weighs us down, thus purifying ourselves. It is a reminder of the *tashlich* service of the High Holidays when we purge ourselves of the transgressions which weigh us down. As Passover approaches we clean our homes of the *chametz,* and we gather it up and burn it prior to the start of the holy day.

Passover calls upon us to remember the seminal historical event of our people—the Exodus, the redemption. It also calls upon us to consider what it is that each one of us can do to secure the redemption of those who are still enslaved in our world. And in a hearkening back to the High Holidays and the tashlich service, we are called to liberate ourselves from the chametz in our lives, those things that weigh us down, hold us back, and prevent us from becoming a better version of ourselves. On this level, Passover is like our mid-year check up. We are reminded to ask ourselves how we are doing with the goals we set for ourselves at Rosh Hashanah and Yom Kippur. How are we doing in our efforts to move closer to hitting the mark, turning back to the right path, and becoming the person we would each like to be?

How am I doing in my journey toward personal redemption and away from that which has weighed me down in the past?

Where have I lost my way on that journey and how can I, as a GPS would say, "recalculate?"

What is one action to which I can commit that will help me return to the right path?

May
Iyar–Sivan

אייר-סיון

There is a tradition that we count the *Omer* between Passover and the following pilgrimage festival, *Shavuot*. We begin the counting on the second night of Passover (at the Seder, for those who have the tradition of a second Seder). Every evening we recite the blessing for counting the Omer and we count the day. For example, we would count: *Today is twenty-two days, which is three weeks and one day of the Omer.*

The commandment is found in the Book of Leviticus (23:15–16), but we are not given much additional information about this commandment. Therefore, as is the way of our people, many layers of meaning have been assigned to this ritual. On the surface it seems to be related to the agricultural year as it is described in the Torah, bridging two harvest times. There are historical aspects which have shaped its observance as well as its more spiritual meaning.

Passover is the celebration and observance of our redemption from slavery. Shavuot, forty-nine days later, is our celebration of accepting the gift of Torah from God. One might think of this as a count down to a special day much the same way we might count down the days to a vacation, to a birthday, wedding, or Bar or Bat Mitzvah. School children often count down the days to summer vacation. One can imagine that God may have said to the Israelites as they began their frightening journey out of Egypt and into the unknown: In forty-nine days I will give you a special gift. And then the Israelites counted day-by-day until the day they were to receive that gift.

The holy days of Judaism are indeed special, but in addition we have the in-between times that lead to those special days. If the holy days are the special events, then the in-between times are the days in the wilderness, the days of journeying, of soul-searching, of growing and maturing. In the case of our Israelite ancestors, they needed that time to begin to grow as spiritual beings now that the shackles of slavery were removed. We too benefit from that in-between time, that time to reflect, to prepare for what may come next. In a way, Shabbat is given to us as that gift. Imagine a week without a day of rest, a day to reflect and step back from a week of working and of everyday creating.

The forty-nine days between Passover and Shavuot now include *Lag b'Omer*, the thirty-third day of the Omer, as well as the remembrance days of *Yom HaZikaron, Yom HaShoah, Yom HaAtzmaut,* and *Yom Yerushalayim*—Israel's Memorial Day, Holocaust Remembrance Day, Israel's Independence Day, and Jerusalem Day. During these seven weeks of counting, we reflect and prepare for the annual acceptance of our Torah, our Tree of Life, our guide for how to live a meaningful life.

How do I benefit from setting aside time to reflect?

How can I intentionally set aside reflection time?

How can I use these in-between days to reflect and help me further the intentions that I set forth during the High Holidays?

June
Sivan–Tammuz

סיון-תמוז

The holy day of Shavuot falls sometime between mid-May and mid-June. After we count forty-nine days from the second night of Passover, the fiftieth day is Shavuot. Depending on one's community and tradition, we observe Shavuot as one or two days. It is marked by the ritual of the *tikkun leil Shavuot*, the all-night study that is a remembrance of our ancestors as they stood anxious and awe-filled awaiting the revelation of Torah at the foot of Mount Sinai. It is a night dedicated to studying Torah and all the texts and wisdom that have been born of it these past thousands of years.

We also mark the holiday with the custom of eating dairy products and reading *Megillat Rut,* the Scroll of Ruth, from the Book of Writings, the third section of the Jewish Bible. Because of the connection to the receiving and accepting of Torah and Ruth's embracing of the covenant, we often mark conversions within our communities as well as adult B'nei Mitzvah and confirmation class graduations at this time.

Shavuot calls upon us to ask: What is my relationship to Torah? Just as on Passover we are each called upon to imagine ourselves as having personally been redeemed from slavery, Shavuot calls us to imagine that each of us personally received and accepted the Torah. According to tradition, every Jewish soul, past, present, and future, stood at the foot of Mount Sinai and was a witness to the revelation of Torah. The Torah was given to the community and to each of us individually.

Jewish tradition considers each of us as a letter of Torah. The Torah would not be complete or fit for use if a letter were to be missing, and similarly, the Jewish community would not be whole or complete without each one of us.

What is my relationship to Torah?

How might the words of Torah and my relationship to it bring me closer to fulfillment of the person I would like to be?

What is my relationship to the Jewish community?

Are there obstacles which get in the way of my strengthening that connection? What might I do to strengthen that bond?

July
Tammuz–Av

תמוז-אב

Shivat-asar b'Tammuz is a fast day in the Jewish calendar which begins at sunrise and ends at nightfall. It is observed on the seventeenth day of the month of Tammuz, deriving its name from the date upon which it is observed. This day marks the beginning of the three week period that culminates in the fast of *Tisha b'Av*, which marks the destruction of both the First and Second Temples in Jerusalem. Tisha b'Av is the only twenty-five hour fast in the Jewish calendar other than Yom Kippur.

In addition to this period between Shivat-asar b'Tammuz and Tisha b'Av, we also mark the time between Tisha b'Av and Rosh Hashanah. On each Shabbat during those seven weeks, we recite a *haftarah* of consolation. We are consoling ourselves and one another over the tragic destruction of both temples (and other tragedies that are said to have taken place on the ninth of Av), and we are preparing ourselves to move into the reflective and spiritual time of the Days of Awe. These are again times between times, periods in the Jewish calendar which are defined by a certain communal tone and mood and, by some, certain observances as well.

Those who observe the days between Shivat-asar b'Tammuz and Tisha b'Av, limit their activities (except on Shabbat) as one might during a time of mourning. Beginning on the first day of the Hebrew month of Av and up to the beginning of the fast day, those observances are intensified, particularly with the observance of eschewing meat (again, with the exception of Shabbat).

When we take on certain observances or limit ourselves, we are choosing to make sacrifices. Just as one might when sitting *shiva* for a loved one, we focus on the internal as opposed to the pleasures of life. One might give up movies, live music, and other activities which typically bring pleasure. Certainly by giving up certain foods such as meat or fasting from eating and drinking for a day, we are making a sacrifice, and by doing so, we are choosing to focus on our spiritual and emotional needs rather than our physical needs.

This is an appropriate time to reflect on the intentions that we each set forward last Rosh Hashanah. We can think about how we have progressed toward our goals and how we have fallen short. It is a good time to consider the sacrifices we have made, those things we have given up in order to bring ourselves closer to the person we have wanted to see when we look in the mirror. It is a time to consider in what ways we have grown and in what ways the sacrifices have benefitted us and proven to be worthwhile.

What have I given up this year?

Has that sacrifice produced a positive yield? In what way?

How might I continue to build on that?

August
Av–Elul

אב-אלול

We have arrived at the end of the year and the beginning of the next year in the Jewish calendar cycle. It was approximately a year ago that we began this journey of self-reflection and introspection prompted by the upcoming High Holidays, and now we are given a fresh opportunity to do the same, to begin again. It is a gift we are given every year at this time.

When we began a year ago, we determined to try to hit a little closer to the bull's-eye, to imagine what we might do to move closer to what God would want of us.

This is an opportunity to reflect on the goals we have each set for ourselves and how we did in our effort toward achieving those goals. How did we each overcome the obstacles or, conversely, why were we unable to overcome them?

One of the challenges we face in setting goals is that while we can anticipate some things in the months to come—a Bar or Bat Mitzvah, a birth, or even the death of a loved one who is critically ill—there are things, of course, that no one can foresee. Sometimes, those surprises become obstacles to achieving our goals, and sometimes they give us the opportunity to practice and use the new tools in our metaphoric toolbox to face those obstacles and to reinforce our strengths through adversity.

As is to be expected at this time of year, we look back over the challenges and achievements and to the ways we have grown. We can acknowledge the ways in which we have increased our sense of self-awareness. We can look at the new relationships which are taking root and the old ones that we have nurtured. We can, as well, mourn those relationships that, through our own choosing or not, have dwindled or died.

We have the opportunity to recognize and celebrate our growth and, at the same time, look to the year ahead and what we may be anticipating. And we look forward to another opportunity to begin again, yet again.

What would I like to change for the upcoming year?

Can I commit to bringing more repentance, prayer, and acts of righteousness into my day-to-day life? Is this something I would like to do? How might I achieve it?

Is there a relationship in my life in need of nurturing? How might I begin to nurture it?

חזק חזק ונתחזק

Chazak Chazak V'nitchazek

Be strong, be strong, and let us be strengthened.

It is an Ashkenazic tradition that as we end the reading of a book of the Torah, the congregation chants together, *Chazak, Chazak, V'nitchazek.* This can be translated: "Be strong, be strong, and let us be strengthened" or "Be strong, be strong, and let us strengthen one another."

As we recite these words as a community, we are praying, expressing hope, resolving to find strength in the words of Torah that we have read together and also in the community we share together.

In a similar way, I invite each of us to take some time now to reflect on the past year in which we have dedicated ourselves to the pursuit of "hitting the mark." We know that self-reflection involves looking at parts of ourselves that perhaps we would prefer not to see and then finding the fortitude, determination, and commitment to take the often challenging steps needed to become a more evolved version of ourselves.

We recognize that sometimes we take these steps alone, forging our own path through what may feel like unknown or unfamiliar territory. Many of us, however, choose to take this journey with the support and encouragement of others, especially those who give us strength along the way.

Whether you have taken this journey alone, in community, or with the support of one or several trusted individuals, it is a journey to celebrate with the recognition that you have grown through your commitment and your effort.

I invite you to take some time and, should you wish, to write about the journey. Celebrate the efforts and the successes and even acknowledge and celebrate the challenging moments as well.

Be strong, be strong, and let us each feel strengthened.

Acknowledgements

I am deeply appreciative to all those who were part of my personal journey from passive congregant to more fully engaged participant in the High Holiday experience with a full appreciation of what Elul and the High Holidays have to offer each of us on a spiritual level as well as toward our personal growth. Many thanks to those who shared their thoughts and ideas as I imagined this book and who, directly or indirectly, contributed to the final product.

I relied on many resources as I imagined and created this book. Each provided information that contributed to the book you are reading. The most precious of these resources are my maternal grandfather Louis Schnell's Rosh Hashanah and Yom Kippur machzorim. These books are my companions every year during the High Holidays, and they have been my daily companions on this journey. The realization of this book is due in no small measure to my love of Judaism which was nurtured by my grandparents Louis and Bess Schnell.

Finally, my deep appreciation to Sapphira Fein and Seth Rosenzweig of Blackbird Books. They were my partners in the birthing of my first book, *On Sacred Ground,* and they have embraced the vision of *For Every Season.* They provided wise counsel and offered invaluable support. Their creative and technical contributions as well as their collaboration and gentle guidance have made this book a more valuable resource. I am appreciative of their partnership and of their generosity of heart and their friendship.

About the Author

Jeff Bernhardt is a Jewish educator and Jewish communal professional, a licensed clinical social worker and writer. His work has been published in anthologies (including *Rosh Hashanah Readings* and *Mentsh*), in the *Los Angeles Times,* as well as in Jewish newspapers throughout the United States. He has written several stage plays (including *Mixed Blessings* and *Therapy*) and dramatic readings which have been used in synagogues and Jewish communal institutions throughout North America. These include *Who Shall Live . . . ?, Standing at Sinai,* and *Those Who Walked Beside Us.* He is also the creator and editor of the book, *On Sacred Ground: Jewish and Christian Clergy Reflect on Transformative Passages from the Five Books of Moses* (Blackbird Books, 2012). He currently resides in Los Angeles and can be reached at jmbedsw@aol.com or through www.jewishdramas.com.

To see our other great titles,
visit us at:

BLACKBIRD BOOKS
www.bbirdbooks.com